TWENTY-FIVE YEARS
BEHIND BARS

WERTHEIM PUBLICATIONS IN INDUSTRIAL RELATIONS

ESTABLISHED IN 1923 BY THE FAMILY OF THE LATE
JACOB WERTHEIM "FOR THE SUPPORT OF ORIGINAL RESEARCH
IN THE FIELD OF INDUSTRIAL COOPERATION."

TWENTY-FIVE YEARS

BEHIND BARS

The Proceedings of the Twenty-fifth anniversary of the U.P.C.

at the Smithsonian Institution, September 30, 1999

Alan L. Haberman, General Editor

PUBLISHED BY THE HARVARD UNIVERSITY
WERTHEIM PUBLICATIONS COMMITTEE
DISTRIBUTED BY HARVARD UNIVERSITY PRESS
CAMBRIDGE, MASSACHUSETTS, AND LONDON, ENGLAND
2001

8764401

KSG- BGP 586

Graphs in "The Diffusion of UCC Standards" courtesy of the Uniform Code Council.

Printed in the United States of America

10 9 8 7 6 5 4 3 2 1

This book is printed on acid-free paper, and its binding materials have been chosen for strength and durability.

ISBN: 0-674-00657-7

CONTENTS

PREFACE

Creativity. Ingenuity. Veracity. Tenacity. It took all that and more to arrive at the global solutions we now call the "Universal Product Code."

As the president and chief executive officer of the Uniform Code Council, I have the honor and privilege of sharing with you our celebration marking the silver anniversary of what I believe is a watershed event in the development of global commerce. The immense magnitude of the impact of this little symbol cannot be overstated. It is at the core of commerce, transportation, warehousing, manufacturing, and retailing, and its influence has spread to virtually every industry sector on the planet.

This book is the record of the proceedings of the daylong symposium that took place at the Smithsonian Institution on September 30, 1999. They look back at how we arrived at this moment in time, the people and pathways that were so instrumental in launching a revolution, and at how one code has begotten a generation of enabling business solutions that will serve us well into the future.

We believe the revolution that was and is the U.P.C. can be a blueprint for the cooperative, focused, multi-sector solutions that will be needed to address our rapidly changing world. We offer this record not only as such a map, but also as a hats off (a place marker of) to what the industrial community can accomplish voluntarily and unaided when there is a clear vision of a better future.

It is my hope that this record will inspire others to collectively meet the economic and societal challenges of technology with talent, teamwork and resolve.

Tom Rittenhouse.
President and C.E.O. of the Uniform Code Council, Inc.

Introduction

In May 1998, the first joint meeting of the Uniform Code Council (UCC) and the EAN International (European Article Numbering Association) took place in Chicago. The day marked the twenty-fifth anniversary of the inauguration of the inter-industry Ad Hoc Committee that became the Uniform Code Council, and the twentieth anniversary of EAN International. More important, it served as the occasion on which the two organizations dedicated themselves to a program of cooperation – indeed – partnership, to harmonize their activities and outputs to create one global system for the worldwide marketplace. Nothing better illustrates the importance and vitality of the identification systems built on the U.P.C. than this response to the needs of their, at the time, 850,000-member business organization. The U.P.C. has developed to the point where it makes it possible to operate in a single distribution channel that need not recognize international borders, language barriers, or legislated trade restraints.

Many of the early players in the U.P.C. movement were invited to the joint meeting activities. Among them grew recognition that the celebration was not complete. A new and revolutionary process of creating and supporting standards had been developed over the twenty-five years of the U.P.C. – a design with meaning far beyond the U.P.C. itself. This voluntary standardization effort has served in many instances, and potentially can serve in even broader movements in the future, to forward the process of standardization for the good of commerce and the consumer. There were people to be honored, events to be memorialized, lessons to be passed on, and futures to be considered in light of the past. With the blessing of Tom Rittenhouse, president and C.E.O. of the

UCC and the promise of funding by the UCC's executive committee, our Major Events Committee was created.

That was the beginning of *Twenty-Five Years Behind Bars,* an all day symposium and dinner jointly sponsored by the UCC and the Smithsonian Institution, which took place in the halls of the Smithsonian's American History Museum on September 30, 1999. It celebrated the silver anniversary of the first commercial scan utilizing the U.P.C. The assembly honored those visionaries who twenty-five years earlier made it possible for that historic package of Wrigley chewing gum to cross the checkout in a Marsh supermarket, and announce its price automatically. But the day's program for the 350 attendees was also very much more than a celebration – it was an occasion for reflection, learning and inspiration.

The morning was devoted to the U.P.C.'s history; analyzing its penetration through industry and inter-industry over time; measuring the results in savings and progress, which far exceeded original expectations; and attempting to extract the process reasons for its success. Following lunch the subject was an examination of the standards process itself: How it fits into history; what we have learned of its many benefits and drawbacks; and the diverse processes that lead to successful standards efforts. Lastly, a mixed panel of practitioners examined the present and future challenges of the U.P.C. and standards in general. The keynote speaker of the evening's celebratory dinner gave a compelling, almost sensational, insider view of what happens within a company when standards development is on the table and its risks and advantages are pursued.

The UCC, mindful of its obligations to its forebears and dedicated to forwarding the process of voluntary standardization as a way for society to control the forces of division and inefficiency, has made this publication possible.

The committee wishes to thank the UCC for its unlimited support and the Smithsonian for its recognition of the U.P.C.'s important place in the technology and commerce of this nation and the world. The speakers and attendees share our thanks and gratitude for making the event a success.

It is to those that learn from and honor the past and move to write an enlightened future that we dedicate this record of the proceedings of the twenty-fifth anniversary of the U.P.C. with the surety that it can be of assistance in their worthy efforts.

The Major Events Committee

Alan L. Haberman, Co-chair
Stephen A. Brown, Co-chair
Fritz Biermeier
Barry Franz
Lawrence C. Russell
Eric Waldbaum
Thomas W. Wilson, Jr.

TWENTY-FIVE YEARS

BEHIND BARS

How a Low-Tech Industry Pulled Off the U.P.C. Standard

Thomas W. Wilson, Jr.

In 1969, members of the Grocery Manufacturers of America and leading retailing associations concluded that there was a need for an "interindustry product code" to reduce the cost of food distribution. The group formed an Ad Hoc Committee of grocery industry executives to cooperatively pursue a uniform grocery product indentification code.

Thomas Wilson's unique perspectives take us through the early history of the Universal Product Code and that of the Uniform Code Council itself, highlighting the core elements of the success of the initiative. He outlines specific reasons why the U.P.C. initiative was successful in a time when so many other industry-sponsored movements failed. Mr. Wilson profiles the key decisions the industry made in conjunction with the U.P.C. project that allowed standards to be formulated and agreed upon.

The development and implementation of the Universal Product Code (U.P.C.) system has been widely hailed as one of the most successful standards-setting efforts ever undertaken. The fact that it was entirely voluntary and conducted solely by private industry makes the effort more remarkable. Most standards-setting efforts have not succeeded.

Before you dismiss me as a pure theorist, let me put into the record my experience on the subject of standards-setting. In 1972, a year before the U.P.C. Symbol standards were published, I assisted Jack Strubbe of Kroger in preparing a presentation to a Pepsi-sponsored industry top management conference in which he theorized on reasons for the apparent early success of the U.P.C. process compared to a dismal industry record on other standards-setting projects. I revisited the subject in the late 1980s at the request of Roger Miliken, who was attempting to move the apparel and textile industry ahead in the areas of logistical efficiency. The subsequent formation of the Voluntary Inter-industry Communications Standards (VICS) committee, whose charter I drafted and on which I served, borrowed heavily from the U.P.C. experience. Finally, I consulted with the European Airline Association in their efforts to automate the passenger ticketing process, was deeply involved in the Direct Product Profit standard, and, like most of you grocery industry "lifers," dealt with ECR and a number of other industry process reform attempts over the years. Thus, I can bring some hands-on experience to this discussion.

The U.P.C. system has been a success. However, it has not been an across-the-board triumph. The original concept of a standard human-readable product code, to be used at all levels in the distribution channel is far from realized, as many retailers still employ their own item numbers, with the U.P.C.'s use limited to point of sale and to Electronic Data Interchange (EDI) communication to vendors. But, the main thrust of U.P.C. – to support front-end automation – has clearly succeeded.

How was it that an industry not known for its prowess in technology was able, in considerably less than ten years, to develop and implement such a massive change? Change, that to be successful, required hundreds of manufacturers to accurately print machine-readable symbols on thousands of individual products, whose packaging spanned dozens of materials printed by a number of very different processes. Change that required thousands of retail outlets to install, operate, and maintain scanning equipment produced by multiple vendors.

I believe there are three fundamental prerequisites for a successful industry standards effort:

1. Skilled executive leadership
2. A viable, demonstrable underlying concept
3. Broad, continuing, industry support.

Why skilled executive leadership? Because, developing and implementing a *voluntary* industry standard is an extraordinarily difficult task, demanding outstanding personal leadership skills. In contrast to top corporate positions, the executive taking on a standards effort lacks the power base provided by corporate law, company bylaws, and economic power. This places a premium on putting highly talented people into these positions. The reality is that too often availability rather than ability governs the selection process. The reasons this is true are fairly obvious. Often, personal and corporate career priorities mitigate against fast-track executives taking on these roles. Also, there is often a degree of conflict and controversy in these efforts that leading other voluntary endeavors (charitable fund raising, for example) does not normally involve. Thus some who are otherwise qualified avoid this activity. In net, lining up the requisite high-level of leadership talent, while critical, is too often not accomplished.

The second prerequisite to success has to do with the underlying concept itself. Standards are clearly "means," not "ends." Yet the temptation for standards setters is to concentrate on the details of the standard rather than on the basic feasibility of the concept. In my view, the majority of failures in industry standards efforts stem from poor basic concepts not flawed standards. Problem identification, in most cases, is done fairly accurately. However, there is frequently an illogical leap from problem to solution, so that after the effort to develop requisite standards is completed, little implementation takes place. And, because many individual industry members must execute the concept, its viability, if not clearly self-evident, must be readily demonstrable.

The final prerequisite to success is the capability to develop broad, continuing industry acceptance and support. Most of us assume that improved industry performance is a widely-shared goal. In fact, in almost all cases there are strong champions of the status quo. This championship may arise from a simple lack of vision or fear of change, but it can also be rooted in a belief that a major change in industry practices will threaten the competitive position of individual participants. Thus, those advocating change must recognize that substantial opposition will emerge and consequently assemble sufficient resources to overcome it. This often raises the practical problem of finding advocates who are committed enough to be willing to take up the fight with dissenters. Trade associations find this difficult, because their memberships often include both camps. In some cases, this role can be played by third parties who see potential economic rewards (e.g. equipment vendors), but they generally suffer from a lack of credibility when advocating "What's good for your industry." At the end of the day, the task of building and maintaining the necessary degree of industry support typically falls on the industry committee/taskforce itself.

It is also true that most major reforms, particularly those involving technology, take longer than initially forecast and frequently require reiteration and revision before finally succeeding. This puts additional pressure on industry advocates to hold the consensus together until the project has developed enough momentum to succeed on its own.

If those are the critical requirements, how did the U.P.C. selection process measure up?

Ad Hoc Committee

Much of the success of the U.P.C. effort traces back to the Ad Hoc Committee. Because standards efforts routinely are managed by industry committees, the formation of the Grocery Industry Ad Hoc Committee on Universal Product Coding in the summer of 1970 hardly qualifies as a seminal event. So, what was different about this one?

Most importantly, it was composed solely of executives who were either the chairman or president of their company – all ten – not just one or two. And, while balanced to include some smaller companies, major players such as General Foods, General Mills, Bristol Myers, H. J. Heinz, SuperValu, A&P, and Kroger were represented. There was equal representation between manufacturers and retailers, five of each, with one retailer being nominated by each of the then five distributor associations. While perhaps politically correct, those balances were far less crucial than the chairman/president qualification for membership. The corporate titles provided the representatives a high degree of protection from parochial interests, allowed them to operate without concern for justifying their actions to any superior, and served effective notice inside and outside the industry that a very serious endeavor was underway.

Adding to the impact of the committee's structure and composition was an agreement to allow members to bring technical advisors from their companies, but to prohibit those advisors from representing the member. The impact of this arrangement was to maintain the level of endeavor at the highest strategic level of total industry focus.

Finally, as should be obvious given the companies involved and the level of representation, the committee benefited from an extraordinary collection of executive talent. As one ocean-racing wag put it at the time, "With that crew, you guys could win the Bermuda Race with *Kon-Tiki*."

A number of benefits resulted from the Ad Hoc Committee's composition. Attendance at meetings was nearly perfect – they made the time. Bill Kane of A&P did miss a meeting while barricaded in his Graybar Building offices by a group of protesters, but that was about it. Early in their deliberations, it became apparent that the members were working hard to see issues from the point of view of their trading partners. This focus became so pronounced that a stranger attending a meeting and attempting to classify manufacturers and retailers by their comments, would be almost totally wrong in his classification. Because the individual members were industry leaders as well, the committee had a built-in power base. Members Burt Gookin and Jim McFarland successively held the chairmanship of the Grocery Manufacturers Association (GMA) from November 1971 through June 1976. When the going got rough, as it inevitably did, the Ad Hoc Committee's political base provided needed strength to push the effort through.

Another defining factor was the committee's charter. While clearly a creature of the six trade associations that had created it, the committee was established with a totally-independent mandate. At its initial meeting, after Heinz C.E.O. Burt Gookin was elected chair, the six trade association executives, (Clancy Adamy, Mike O'Connor, George Koch,

Gerry Peck, Frank Register and Earl Madsen), all rose and left the room in a symbolic gesture of their putting the industry's efforts in the hands of this group.

I am unaware of any other voluntary industry standards movement with a comparable leadership committee arrangement. As to how this brilliant stroke was conceived, I am less certain. I, however, would conclude that such a blue-ribbon committee made an enormous difference in the U.P.C. project's success. I would also conclude that the real trick will be figuring out how to replicate that experience in an era of increased litigation, and one when projects often lack the inherent appeal of front-end automation.

Validating the Concept

The second major factor contributing to the success of the U.P.C. effort was the methodologies employed to first validate the concept of front-end automation based on machine-readable symbols placed on each product. It is my belief that the inclusion of these methodologies in the processes that the Ad Hoc Committee established to govern its deliberations and conclusions was key, not only to its making the correct decisions regarding the desirability of the industry pursuing the concept, but also to the building of an industry consensus to support the committee's recommendations. That consensus ultimately proved strong enough to overcome the obstacles that threatened to postpone or derail widespread implementation.

An important initial step was agreement to the hypothesis that front-end scanning was not necessarily a viable concept. It may seem obvious to first justify the concept and then indentify the necessary standards, but time after time, industry standards efforts fail to follow this route. Typically, advocates get caught up in an initial wave of optimism, accept potential benefits as realizable, and move on to "getting the job done." In the case of the U.P.C., the committee members had an early, collective belief in the principle that net economic benefit to the industry had to be demonstrated before the concept could be accepted. It was perhaps fortunate that costs and benefits were not generated at the same points in the distribution channel. That is, it was quickly seen that symbol marking, if it were to be economically accomplished, had to be done during the product manufacturing process and at the manufacturer's cost. Conversely, while checkout automation was believed to be in the best interests of the entire industry, most of the initial benefits were likely to accrue on the retailer side. Thus, it was not enough for a potential scanner purchaser to calculate whether projected savings at retail justified the cost of the equipment (as is the case in most automation decisions). The upstream cost of making products scannable, which would be passed on to the retailer, needed to be taken into account as well. And, while source marking costs were thought to be modest, one of the earliest realities was that the product of any number above zero, when multiplied by 300 billion (the then item throughput of the industry) was significant. Thus, a collective, cross-industry comparison of costs and benefits was seen to be required in order to reach a conclusion on the economic viability of point-of-sale automation.

Once the Ad Hoc Committee reached this conclusion, it moved to make sure the concept validation process was well executed. The major requirements were time and money. There was strong industry pressure to move ahead with decisions on code and symbol composition rather than continuing with concept justification. Lengthening the feasibility stage two to three times longer than originally announced, along with the accompanying exhaustion of initial association-provided funding was not easy.

Another common failure in justifying the concepts underlying standards development projects is to spend most of the justification effort on the proposed new process and little on what it would replace. Many times, existing performance parameters are developed from a quick collection of industry experience, with ready acceptance of what "everybody knows" and little, if any, confirming analysis. This leads to a number of problems when it comes time to convince skeptics that the new solution is superior. "I don't know where you got those numbers," "our experience is different," and similar rejoinders are bound to emerge. At the time, the belief was that the range of front-end throughput across well-regarded operators using manual checkstands was signifiantly greater than the mean difference in performance between scanning and conventional point-of-sales devices. To deal with these issues, the U.P.C. effort included the development of a parametric model covering every aspect of product movement through the warehouse and retail stages. The model could be run on a conventional basis, with manual checkout, so that it was possible to tie any individual retailer's reported performance to a set of product handling coefficients that were nearly impossible to dispute. Similarly, an advanced case simulation could be run, with agreed upon changes in the relevant coefficients. This allowed the clearest possible layout of the supporting assumptions, leading to a conclusion that the improvements generated by automation were of a specific magnitude for a specific operator. While perhaps obvious today, the task of gaining agreement to and building the parametric model – well before the era of spreadsheet software – was far from easy. Yet it was fundamental to the U.P.C. effort's success.

Anticipation of Dissent

There is a tendency in industry reform efforts to assume, that if an improvement concept is demonstrably worthwhile, support will naturally follow. Actual experiences suggests otherwise. What tends to occur is an initial outpouring of concurrence and enthusiasm, which then fades as the realities of implementation are faced. If unrealistic timetables have been established, the resulting delays tend to fan the flames of dissent and enthusiasm begins to wane. Statements starting with "Of course we still believe in scanning, but. . ." are made, followed by such charges as, "Is the industry ready for it?" "Can we afford it?"and "Don't most of the benefits accrue to 'them' (any constituency other than the audience's)?"

The U.P.C. effort faced these. A few were publicized; most were not. The infamous *Business Week* article in 1976 with its eye-catching headline, "The Scanner that Failed" provides a painful reminder of what the effort faced in the area of eroding support. *Business Week*'s report that the industry was not embracing the new technology – including installation of equipment – on a quick enough or large enough scale, begged the question as to whether the efforts were a failure or a challenge.

The committee needed to define those who might oppose checkout automation. To start, union labor leaders who, not surprisingly, were concerned about loss of membership. Then, existing mechanical cash register producers, store door delivery vendors convinced that "When retailers find out how slowly some of my items actually sell, I'll lose half my distribution," an industry member with an investment in an alternative technology, or an association executive tired of having his nose rubbed into how successful the committee had been – There are always champions of the status quo.

What allowed the U.P.C. effort to succeed against this opposition was an extensive investment in identifying, analyzing and preparing to deal with major issues before they arose. The committee made a major effort to build a broad and deep level of support across the industry. In its efforts to anticipate and deal with dissent, the Ad Hoc Committee:

- Established a so-called "Washington Strategy" sub-committee under the leadership of Gavin McBain, chairman of Bristol-Myers. They developed an issue list, conferred with association executives (grocery industry and others, such as computer manufacturers) and initiated action programs as appropriate to be able to immediately deal with individual problems as they emerged. Examples would be laser beam safety and the perception of disproportionate benefits to larger retailers. In the latter case, a project was initiated to study the potential effects of scanning in smaller stores. Live data was gathered from a dozen or so outlets with sales ranging from $10,000 to $30,000 per week. ($40,000 per week was the average turnover in those days). Utilizing the parametric model mentioned earlier, costs and benefits were projected, and a report developed for use in discussions with the National Association of Retail Grocers in the United States (NARGUS), the National-American Wholesale Grocers Association (NAWGA) and the Cooperative Food Distributors of America (CFDA) leadership. Similar projects were initiated in the areas of packaging costs, consumer shelf-price awareness, and printing tolerances. These were costly undertakings, which a less committed committee might easily have skipped.
- Undertook an initiative to unrestrictedly share its findings with the Retail Clerks Union. Presentations were made to each of three regional meetings of all of the union's locals, and the potential reduction in front-end labor hours was openly shared with them.
- A public policy sub-committee, under Wegman's chairman Bob Wegman, was put in place to carry on the efforts of the Washington Strategy group as the Ad Hoc Committee passed the mantle to the Code Council board.

9

- Prior to the public announcement (scheduled for May 1971) of the committee's initial findings and recommendations to the industry, individual presentations were made to each of some thirty industry member companies, covering both retailers and manufacturers. A precondition of the meeting was that the company's C.E.O. be present (it was left to the C.E.O. as to who else would be invited to attend). An agenda was distributed, which included a list of questions to be asked of the C.E.O. at the conclusion of the meeting. (Do you agree with our findings; are you comfortable with announcing them now, or should the committee do more study before the announcement; if the cost of symbol marking turns out to be consistent with these projections, will your company implement source marking?)

In retrospect, some of these activities may seem like overkill. However, most of those who were closely involved with the U.P.C. effort will tell you that the line between success and failure, or at least substantial delay and less than full realization of potential benefits, was very, very thin.

Intangible

The intangible that contributed to making the U.P.C. development and implementation effort a success was that the concept had a nearly mystical element. It repeatedly captured and challenged the intellectual capabilities of a series of extremely talented individuals, and caused them to become not just supporters but devoted disciples to seeing its potential realized. Jack Strubbe, of Kroger, not only provided much of the behind-the-scenes fuel which powered the effort, but on at least two occasions disregarded the strong advice of company superiors and took actions he felt were necessary for U.P.C.'s success. Because Strubbe was technically competent and had deep knowledge about distribution and food marketing, he was an early conceptualist for technology being used to reinvent the way the industry operated. Additionally, as a patent attorney, he knew about creating standards and dealing with high-tech companies. Albert Heijn of Royal Ahold heard Burt Gookin's presentation at the May 1971 Supermarket Institute (SMI) conference, stepped forward and volunteered to assist in seeing that the European-based industry shared in the benefits of automation. For the next fifteen years he devoted an enormous amount of time and effort, as well as his own reputation, to seeing his vision come true. Gookin, Wegman, Jim Cooke of Penn Fruit, Bob Schaberle, the chairman of the board of Nabisco, Alan Haberman, C.E.O. of Finast, and others, backed actions that seemed to be at odds with their career or company interests. And they did it in the interest of seeing the bar code become a reality. I have had nearly every member of the ad hoc and supporting committees tell me upon their industry retirement that they consider involvement with U.P.C. the most satisfying single accomplishment of their careers.

That is it, then: one active participant's ideas on how a bunch of catsup peddlers and meat cutters succeeded in enabling a set of potentially advantageous technological advances to become an indispensable element in worldwide commerce. To those of you who participated, my congratulations; to those who may attempt similar endeavors, my hopes that these remarks may make a terribly difficult undertaking a little easier.

THE DIFFUSION OF UCC STANDARDS

JOHN T. DUNLOP

BEYOND DEFINING BUSINESS GUIDELINES FOR INDUSTRY, STANDARDS ORGANIZATIONS ARE FACED WITH THE DAUNTING TASK OF GAINING INDUSTRY ACCEPTANCE AND ENABLING BENEFICIARIES TO REALIZE THE POTENTIAL OF STANDARDS USE. PROFESSOR DUNLOP ANALYZES THE MONTHLY GROWTH OF UCC MEMBERSHIP IN TOTAL AND BY PRODUCT CLASSIFICATION. THIS RECORD OF THE INITIAL DIFFUSION, COMBINED WITH THE PUBLICLY AVAILABLE INFORMATION ON THE GROWTH OF INSTALLATIONS IN GROCERY RETAIL STORES, YIELDS ONE OF THE FIRST QUANTITATIVE STUDIES OF NETWORK EXTERNALITIES. AS HE POINTS OUT, THE STANDARD SUCCEEDED BECAUSE OF THE STRONG INDUSTRY LEADERSHIP PROMOTING A CONFLUENCE OF CONCEPT, EQUIPMENT, AND INSTALLATIONS. IT ALSO ILLUSTRATES AN "S"-CURVE PATTERN OF GROWTH RATES THAT SHOWS SUCCESSSIVE INDUSTRY GROUPS REACHING SATURATION AND NEW GROUPS MAKING THE DECISON TO AUTOMATE WITH U.P.C.

HE SPEAKS ABOUT WHY BAR CODING AND RELATED DISTRIBUTION TECHNOLOGIES ARE CLEARLY AMONG THE GREAT INNOVATIONS OF THE LAST QUARTER OF THE TWENTIETH CENTURY AND WHY THE SECOND TWENTY-FIVE YEARS MAY BE THE MOST EXCITING FOR THE U.P.C. HE MAKES FIVE OBSERVATIONS THAT POINT TO THAT FUTURE: THE NEW FORM OF INTERINDUSTRY RELATIONS THE U.P.C. ENABLED; THE PRODUCTITIVTY SAVINGS GENERATED AND DISTRIBUTED; THE UTILIZATION GAPS THAT REMAIN AND THE MAJOR POTENTION THEY OFFER; U.P.C.'S ROLE IN THE WIDER "INFORMATION INTEGRATED CHANNEL" THAT CHALLENGES MANAGEMENT CAPABILITIES; AND LAST, HE GIVES RECOGNITION TO THE ROLE OF VOLUNTARY SECTORAL COOPERATION IN CREATING EFFICIENICES.

On June 21–22, 1994 the UCC Board of Governors met at the Harvard Business School to hear a panel of Harvard and MIT professors on the "Future of Technology and Implications for UCC," which was followed by a board review of its mission/objectives. At that meeting we learned of a manuscript in process by Stephen A. Brown on the origins of the U.P.C. Published in 1997, his authoritative narrative, *Revolution at the Checkout Counter* was an important step in the diffusion of information about U.P.C. and its origins.

Diffusion in Aggregate Registrations

At our request, UCC placed its paper records of applications, with attendant information, on computer disks for the period from the outset to 1984 and furnished us these tapes for our analysis, initially for the period ending in 1994. More recently the data through 1998 were made available. We are grateful to UCC for use of these distinctive data sets.

Figure 1 displays the truly exponential growth of cumulative U.P.C. registrations in the 1971–1998 period on an annual basis. Figure 2 shows the annual U.P.C. registrations in the same period, reflecting the

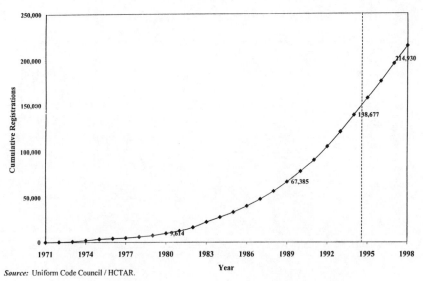

Source: Uniform Code Council / HCTAR.

Figure 1: Annual Cumulative U.P.C. Registrations, 1971–1998.

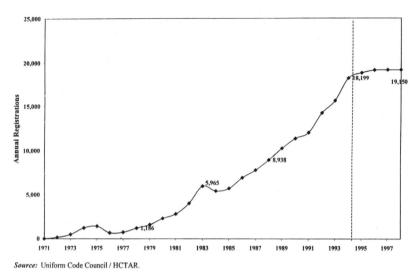

Source: Uniform Code Council / HCTAR.

Figure 2: Annual U.P.C. Registrations, 1971–1998.

retardation in the annual growth rate of U.P.C. registrations in the years since the mid-1990s. Figure 3 reflects the total U.P.C. registrations on a monthly basis for 1971–1998 with the jagged seasonal pattern, showing the same recent retardation or "S-shape" in growth rates.

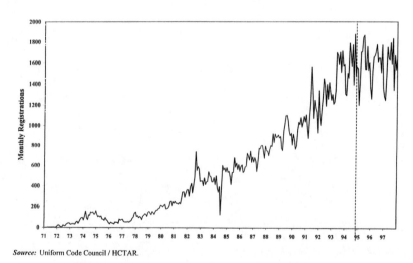

Source: Uniform Code Council / HCTAR.

Figure 3: Monthly Total U.P.C. Registrations, 1971–1998.

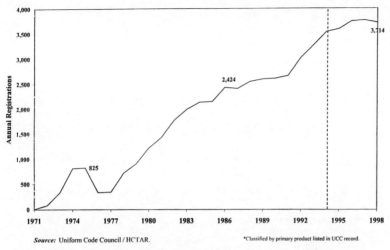

Source: Uniform Code Council / HCTAR.   *Classified by primary product listed in UCC record.

*Figure 4: Food and Beverage U.P.C. Registrations, 1971–1998.**

As in the case of the diffusion of many technologies, the retardation after 1994 or "S-shape" in U.P.C. total registrations arose from the "saturation" of bar codes in many consumer product segments. Further, growth depends on additional product proliferation, ongoing new entrants and exits from an industry, and new consumer-oriented segments. This pattern of adoption and diffusion in specific product segments is illustrated in Figures 1 through 4.

Diffusion by Primary Product

The original registrations in groceries led to the dominance of "food and beverage" products in the early years. In 1975, 64.3 percent of all registrations were in food and beverage, compared to 4.3 percent in housewares and 3.5 percent in beauty aids and a wide scattering of primary product listed in the registration applications. By 1994, food and beverage products only constituted 28.4 percent of all registrations as bar codes and related technologies diffused throughout domestic distribution.

The patterns of growth in registrations by primary product over the years since the 1970s is instructive as to developments in the adoption of distribution technologies by sectors. A few figures by primary product

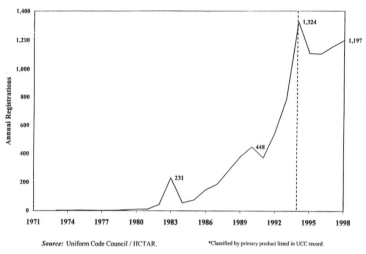

Source: Uniform Code Council / HCTAR.   *Classified by primary product listed in UCC record.

*Figure 5: Apparel Industry U.P.C. Registrations, 1971–1998.**

may be useful in making the point against the backdrop of the pattern in food and beverage. Figure 4 shows food and beverage U.P.C. registrations, the early source of registrations, with the declines in 1975–1976 and the steady expansion thereafter.

The apparel and retail industry story in Figure 5, has been of special interest on account of the size and developments of the sector and a major research project with the recent publication of *A Stitch in Time.** Registrations became significant in 1983 and in the late 1980s with the adoption of these technologies by Kmart and Wal-Mart. It was not a concern with front-end costs or productivities, but the management of inventories, product proliferation, replenishments and mark-downs that attracted department stores which imposed "lean retailing" procedures on their suppliers.

Figures 6 and 7 reflect the patterns of growth in registration in two other sectors – building supplies/home improvement and the computer (hard/soft). These data reflect internal developments and competitive factors in these sectors, data for much doctoral research.

*Frederick H. Abernathy, John T. Dunlop, Janice H. Hammond, David Weil, *A Stitch in Time: Lean Retailing and the Transformation of Manufacturing – Lessons from the Apparel and Textile Industries,* New York: Oxford University Press, 1999.

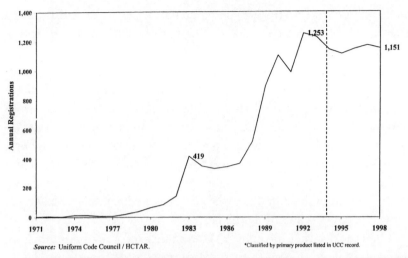

Figure 6: Building Supplies/Home Improvement U.P.C. Registrations, 1971–1998.*

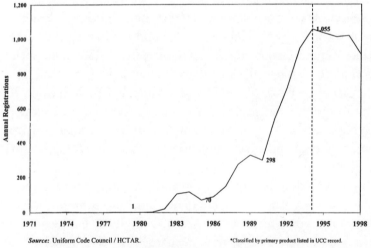

Figure 7: Computer (Hard/Soft) U.P.C. Registrations, 1971–1998.*

The Initial and Critical Diffusion

In Revolution at the Checkout Counter Stephen Brown identifies what he calls a classic "chicken and egg" dilemma: "Why would a retailer invest in scanning equipment until a significant amount of his product was source coded? Why should a manufacturer go to the trouble of source coding

17

product if there were no retailers prepared to scan it?" Economists have a fancier name for these issues, and elaborate theory, to identify the problem – network externalities.

The Ad Hoc Committee, and its Symbol Selection Sub-Committee early on recognized these network externalities. Scanners – the hardware – had little value until the U.P.C. symbol – the software – was commonplace. Conversely, the symbol was of limited use unless scanners were installed. The system as a whole would not yield net savings, the pioneers believed, until 75 percent of products bore the symbol and scanners were installed in nearly 8,000 supermarkets. The personal leadership of the Ad Hoc Committee played a major role in the achievement of these objectives – a critical diffusion.

The Food Market Institute (FMI) monthly records of grocery store installations of scanners, from 1974 through 1985 and the UCC monthly data of cumulative manufacturers applying for the U.P.C. have permitted one of the first quantitive studies of network externalities.*

The effect of bar code adoptions by manufacturers on the adoption of checkout scanners by retailers was large and reinforcing during this early period. Zimmerman found that each increase of 1,350 manufacturers adopting U.P.C. bar codes increased the probability of retail adoption of scanners by a factor of ten. Over the same time period, when 360 more retail stores adopted scanners, the probability of further adoption of U.P.C. bar codes among remaining manufacturers increased by one third. These interaction effects underlie the pattern of registrations depicted in the figures.

Those involved in the introduction and diffusion of new technologies generally in the economy need to understand and confront issues of these externalities for which the lessons of U.P.C. are instructive. For example, a wide variety of information technologies employed by "lean retailers" and the widely discussed group of "e-tailers" employ technologies whose benefits grow as other businesses adopt related technologies or

---

*Gary Efrem Zimmerman, "The Effects of Network Externalities on the Adoption of the Universal Adoption of the Universl Product Code: An Empirical Investigation of Grocery Retailers and Manufacturers, 1970–80," Harvard Undergraduate Honors Thesis, March 1999.)

procedures. Illustrations include electronic data interchange and associated software platforms, advanced shipping notification, financial/accounting software, and product display standards.

European Developments

By the 1960s and 1970s, prior to the formation of the Food Marketing Institute in 1976, the leading European supermarket organizations regularly participated in the activities of the Supermarket Institute (SMI), the National Association of Food Chains (NAFC), Grocery Manufacturers Association (GMA), and other trade associations. As Stephen Brown notes, first hand reports on the progress of U.P.C. were regularly available to these European organizations.

When Albert Heijn, C.E.O. of Royal Ahold, the Dutch supermarket company, concluded that the American experience could be applied in Europe, a European analog to the Ad Hoc Committee was formed and to which McKinsey & Company and Tom Wilson also provided consulting help. There had already been some separate parallel experiments. Migros in Switzerland was testing a scanner with a half bull's-eye symbol at about the same time that Kroger was testing scanning with a bull's-eye symbol.

The European Article Numbering Association, (EAN), as the European code and symbol were called, was unveiled in mid-1976. To accommodate coding authorities of other nations, EAN added an extra digit at the beginning of the code denoting the country. As Dr. A. Heijn reports, the EAN Ad Hoc Committee decided that the same technology as U.P.C. would be used for EAN but with thirteen digits, and more capacity was created. The U.P.C. and EAN systems thus became compatible. All U.P.C. symbols can be scanned in the EAN environment. A sunset date of 2005 has now been set for the change of the U.P.C. 12-digit and the EAN 13-digit symbols to a single 14-digit symbol, thus increasing capacity and improving compatibility.

Just as UCC grew far beyond its origins in the United States grocery industry, so too has EAN expanded its territory. In May 1997 the UCC Board of Governors for the very first time hosted the EAN

General Assembly. The Uniform Code Council, Inc. annual report for 1998 begins with the following euphoric pronouncement:

> It was a watershed event that opened the doors to an unprecedented cooperation in the quest for one global system for the worldwide marketplace. . . . A universal language is now rapidly emerging in the open standards, shared technologies and applied business strategies of the global EAN-UCC system. Today, in over 140 nations around the world, supply chain partners are finding common ground in the identification and electronic exchange of information related to products, services, transport units, assets, and locations. Worldwide, more than 800,000 member companies across virtually every industry sector have formed a critical mass of users. . . . And more than 5 billion scanning transactions a day testify to the power and potential behind the new global language of business.

Diffusion Processes

From the creation of the Ad Hoc Committee and the Symbol Selection Subcommittee more than a quarter century ago, we have seen a continuing expanding universe:

1. The initial diffusion was to achieve the critical level of Stephen Brown's "chicken and egg" problem or the network externalities of scanners, marking of grocery products, and the installation of the checkout counters.
2. The diffusion throughout the Food and Beverage sector has been steady with associated product proliferation, much larger stores and the addition of numerous new departments and an approach to the early objective of one-stop shopping.
3. The diffusion to department stores, and other types of retail outlets has its own patterns with emphasis on the more effective management of inventories and their risks.

4. The diffusion internationally has been an ongoing feature of the expansion commenced by the "founding fathers."

Elements of an Assessment

In the Introduction to Stephen Brown's *Revolution at the Checkout Counter*, I expressed the judgment that "bar coding and related distribution technologies are clearly among the great innovations of the last quarter of this century, and the full impact of these technologies is yet to be felt." A few observations in support of the judgment are in order.

1. The U.P.C. standards facilitate relations among independent enterprises and households at different levels of the distribution system – manufacturers, suppliers, retailers, consumers – that were previously only related by entirely independent markets. In the new world a channel is created from various suppliers and intermediaries through to retailers and households tied together by information technologies and standards. There are new forms of interfirm relations, communications and business practices, and new interactions with consumers. There are new boundaries and dimensions to enterprises. No two channels are precisely the same. This is a new real world, and a new one as well for economic model-builders.

2. In these new production and distribution channels to consumers there are sources of overall money savings, enhanced productivity, reduced risks of holding inventories, and reduced time for transactions. These aggregate economics may be shared differently among the participants in the channel. But enhanced savings, productivities, risk reduction, and time saving seems clear despite the difficulties of precise measurement.

   As long ago as 1995, Federal Reserve Chairman Alan Greenspan said, "In the business sector, the traditional practice of holding inventories . . . at a wide range of locations in the chain of distribution is being revolutionized, and lines of demarcation between retailer, wholesaler, and manufacturer are being blurred, the potential grows for custom design of products suited to particular tastes of individual consumers."*

On June 14, 1999 in his testimony before the Joint Economic Committee, Chairman Alan Greenspan further stated: "But the recent years' remarkable surge in the availability of real-time information has enabled business management to remove large swaths of inventory "safety stocks" and worker redundancies, and has armed firms with detailed data to fine-tune product specifications to most individual customer needs." Then he refers to bar codes: "Information access in real-time – resulting, for example, from such processes as checkout counter bar code scanning and satellite location of trucks – has fostered marked reduction in delivery lead-times on all sorts of goods, from books to capital equipment."

3. There are immense gaps in the present state of affairs and how much more is possible. The long period that it took food distribution to move beyond the economies of the front-end checkout to inventory and category management is only one illustration.

A recent study at Iowa State University of non-chain apparel retailers in sixteen states showed eighty percent of the respondents had gross sales under one million dollars a year. The vast majority of respondents – 89 percent – used a cash register for their retail operations, although only 15 percent used registers equipped with bar coding capability, and only 26 percent tied their registers into inventory management. Three-quarters of the respondents did not use SKUs for their business . . . although most respondents, 69 percent, used a computer for their business activities.*

*Remarks before the Gerald R. Ford Foundation and the Economic Club of Grand Rapids, Michigan, November 7, 1995.
*Bonita Marett Langreck, "Computer Technology Adoption by Small Apparel Retailers: A Network Perspective," M.Sc. Thesis, Iowa State University, 1999.

Thus the significant arena of small business is a frontier for adaptations of standards, technologies and savings. This is a major challenge.

4. We use the term "information integrated channels" to stress that it is the full compliment of information technologies and related processes in combination that is the source of time savings, management of risks, increased productivity and economies. It is not bar codes alone nor scanners, but it is the information integrated channel comprised of bar codes, scanners, electronic data interchange (EDI), automated distribution centers, and standards for packing and delivery – all appropriate to the channel – that makes the difference. The mix and specialized standards will vary with the particular channel from supplier to retailer and consumer. No one innovation is enough.

A study of apparel and retailing, *A Stitch in Time,* shows that enterprises adopting the full complex of technologies do in fact have lower inventories with their associated risks and higher profitability. The study establishes "that an economy characterized by an increasing level of modern manufacturing and retailing practices should experience lower levels of inventories relative to sales. . . . This is important because aggregate inventory volatility has historically made up a significant portion of GDP volatility. The macroeconomic link may prove to be the most profound implication of the adoption of firm-level information technology and workplace practices."*

The study of the apparel-retail channel showed that business units that did not adopt any of the four key practices – bar codes, Electronic Data Interchange (EDI), advanced shipping systems, and modular assembly – earned the lowest profit margins – about 3 percent in 1992. The most

---

*Margaret Hwang and David Weil, "Who Holds the Bag: The Impact of Workplace Practices and Information Technologies on Inventories," Proceedings of the 50th Annual Meeting of the Industrial Relations Research Association, Madison, Wisconsin, 1998, pp. 68–77.

innovative firms using all practices were approximately four times as profitable, achieving average profit margins of 11.7 percent.

There is considerable opportunity ahead to have partial adopters of information technologies complete their investment in full-integrated channels or else yield market share to those who have invested in the full compliment. Research with retailers and manufacturers reports that full "channel integration" entails many severe managerial difficulties.

5. A noteworthy feature of the "founding fathers" and U.P.C. was the process of setting industry standards without government intervention or regulation, particularly from 1971–1974, when regulation was so pervasive in the food sector.* The course of the "founding fathers" is to be highly commended. The incentives were there; the front-end of the supermarket was a major opportunity in many ways, and the time to achieve results did not require a government regulatory structure. While I do not believe all standards of manufacture and commerce can be set by industry alone, as in the case of wireless channels and pharmaceutical safety standards, there is much to commend the sectoral cooperation, the technical and business collaboration, and the remarkable foresight of the Ad Hoc Committee and its Symbol Selection Subcommittee in the early 1970s.

The development of the U.P.C. can be compared with the Admiral of the Ocean Sea – Columbus. He sought the Indies and Japan and instead found Guanaharrí, which he renamed San Salvador, that became a part of a New World. The U.P.C. "founding fathers" sought front-end savings in food chain stores that grew into the new world of information integrated channels for all distribution.

---

*John T. Dunlop and Kenneth J. Fedor, ed., *The Lessons of Wage and Price Controls – The Food Sector,* Boston: Division of Research, Graduate School of Business Administration, Harvard University, 1997.

Scanning's Silver Celebration

John E. Nelson

The Ad Hoc Committee's management of the business case for the Univerasl Produce Code is an instructive lesson for today's business community. The economic benefits of the U.P.C. had to be large enough to drive investment and conservative enough to stand up to the inevitable skepticism that would be leveled from the beginning.

Representatives of the Uniform Code Council asked PricewaterhouseCoopers to prepare a report detailing contributions the U.P.C. has made to industry, to international economies, and to the consuming public through the first twenty-five years. As a representative of PricewaterhouseCoopers, John Nelson presents the research finding by painting a clear picture of how the symbol has stood up to the original business case. The report, titled "17 Billion Reasons to Say Thanks: 25 Years of the U.P.C. and Its Impact on the Grocery Industry," shows how well the work of the Ad Hoc Committee has paid off.

What an impact the U.P.C. has had on our lives! The products that we want to buy are in the stores where we want to shop, at a fair price, just when we want to buy them. Because we have the U.P.C., we can quickly scan products at the checkout, we know what our stock levels are, and we can efficiently deliver goods directly to the store. Let's take a look at how amazingly innovative the U.P.C. really was, and is. Let's look at the themes that the Smithsonian exhibit will reflect this evening; the effects on society and the technological advancements that the U.P.C. has inspired; and let's take a quick retrospective look all the way from the original U.P.C. business case, to where the technology has brought us today – and what's on the horizon.

Innovation through uniformity? It sounds like a nonsequitor. Today, we think of uniformity as uninspiring, but uniformity was nothing short of innovation twenty-five years ago in retailing. Remember what shopping was like without uniformity? I remember searching through the cans on the shelf, looking for the peas with the lowest price, because somebody hadn't gone around and stamped the new price. I remember the embarrassing wait in the checkout line when my price sticker fell off my frozen box of beans and somebody had to run back and look in the freezer for it. We know where the savings are coming from. It's the other end of the experience; it's the retailers and manufactures' memories.

The retailers do have memories. They remember the armies of stock clerks stamping prices on every candy bar, and then restamping them when the next sale came along – every one of them! They remember the checkout clerks trying to read the handwritten pricing on those packages of T-bone steak, and reading $1.45 instead of $4.45, and losing three dollars on every sale. And they remember taking endless inventories; filling out paper reorder pads so that they'd know how much to reorder; and the huge amount of counting that went on as merchandise was received in the stores. All that tedious effort!

And the manufacturers remember. They remember receiving all those paper orders through the mail. Processing the returns and reductions when we didn't ship exactly what the customer had asked for because we couldn't keep track of all the customer's numbering schemes, and we transcribed those orders incorrectly as they came in the door.

And remember how difficult it was to track all the inventory in our warehouses as it was picked and loaded onto our customer's trucks?

The U.P.C. really is the great enabler – the key to unlocking an enormous amount of information that makes all our jobs easier, and our lives simpler. The U.P.C. did change retailing as we know it. The very concept and implementation of the U.P.C. was an essential building block for retail's rapid expansion, not just in my grocery examples, but in an amazing variety of product categories and retail segments. And while the initial scope of the U.P.C. was focused in the United States, the concept and standards are truly global, one that makes global commerce, even e-commerce, possible today. As we look at the economic effects of the U.P.C., we must remember the tremendous effort and courage required to launch it, and to think about how we can recapture some of that same spirit as we attack today's industry standards and challenges. Think about what can be accomplished when there really is a spirit of partnership to transform the entire industry. Here is how the industry transformation by the U.P.C. has occurred so far.

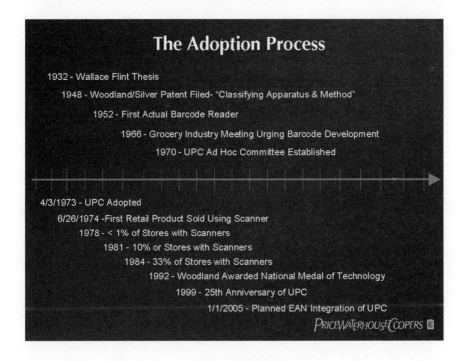

The Adoption Process

1932 - Wallace Flint Thesis

1948 - Woodland/Silver Patent Filed- "Classifying Apparatus & Method"

1952 - First Actual Barcode Reader

1966 - Grocery Industry Meeting Urging Barcode Development

1970 - UPC Ad Hoc Committee Established

4/3/1973 - UPC Adopted

6/26/1974 -First Retail Product Sold Using Scanner

1978 - < 1% of Stores with Scanners

1981 - 10% or Stores with Scanners

1984 - 33% of Stores with Scanners

1992 - Woodland Awarded National Medal of Technology

1999 - 25th Anniversary of UPC

1/1/2005 - Planned EAN Integration of UPC

PRICEWATERHOUSECOOPERS

The seminal concepts of an automated grocery checkout system go as far back as 1948 – the year Dewey defeated Truman. By 1965, Kroger and RCA had pioneered an automated front-end system test. At the same time the development of a relatively cheap laser technology and integrated circuits brought the technology within practical reach of the entire food industry. Kroger's success sparked the industry to take the next step. Technology limitations actually channeled us into uniformity. Since the technology of the time couldn't support reading multiple bar code formats, the question of which bar code standard to choose became a critical issue. Since there were multiple and competing alternatives, as well as divergent interests between the manufacturers and retailers, uniformity became a mandate.

On August 25, 1970, representatives from the cooperative food distributors, the Grocery Manufacturers of America, the National American Wholesale Grocers Association, the National Association of Food Chains, the National Association of Retail Grocers, and the Supermarket Institute came together to form the Ad Hoc Committee.[1] Never has a group with such a modest name accomplished work of such great consequence. Their task was to resolve both the complex business issues and the difficult technical issues, and resolve them they did with the adoption of the symbol in 1973, and the first store installation at one of Marsh's Supermarkets in 1974. The U.P.C. had been born, and Wrigley's chewing gum was the first product to be scanned. The individuals who made up the initial Ad Hoc Committee, took an enormous challenge. Essentially the committee would reshape the way in which business would be conducted beginning with the food industry.

The Ad Hoc Committee was intentionally comprised of six companies representing distribution and retail, and six companies representing the manufacturers. The work of the committee focused on two priorities – the business case and the technical requirements. Burt Gookin of the H. J. Heinz Company chaired the Committee, which focused on building the business case around the economic potential of scanning. It created two subcommittees: Robert Stringer of General Foods chaired the Code Management Sub-committee, and Alan Haberman of First National Stores chaired the Symbol selection committee. Together these two sub-

---

[1]See page 145 for the members of the committee.

committees worked diligently to create a standard that would survive the tough scrutiny of multiple competing constituencies.

There were many obstacles faced by the Ad Hoc Committee. Because the committee took care to understand the enormity of their task, they worked hard to address the needs of many, varied groups. For instance, prior to the U.P.C.'s adoption, some worried that only the larger, more financially endowed competitors would benefit from the uniformity of the U.P.C. What resulted was a much greater benefit than even they had imagined. Initially the Ad Hoc Committee estimated that implementing the U.P.C. would save the industry $1.43 billion in hard benefits. In fact, the actual net benefits today are 5.65 percent of sales within the grocery channel. The channel scans about $293 billion in volume each year, for an annual savings of just under $17 billion annually, just in the grocery channel. These are 1999 numbers. That's an amazing number.*

Consider for a moment trying to balance the concerns of retailers and manufacturers. On one hand, retailers wanted a short code, easy to key if the symbol didn't scan. On the other hand, manufacturers wanted a longer code, which could contain more information and provide greater accuracy. Initially, manufacturers bore the cost of printing the symbol with no assurance the retailers would ever use it. Similarly, the retailers who wanted the benefits of scanning, had to trust that a critical mass of manufacturers would embrace the code, in order to justify their capital costs. Given these concerns, developing these business issues became a principle concern.

Perhaps the biggest obstacle to overcome was sheer inertia. There were many who believed that the change only opened up the field for more competition, and they were threatened by changes not fully understood. And there were threats from outside the industry. Anti-trust concerns were raised here in Washington, and consumer advocates and unions fought any attempt to remove individual item pricing. But the benefits of scanning are not confined only to the grocery industry. If we take into consideration other channels like discount, drug, club, convenience supercenters, we believe there is another $248 billion in scan volume. Assuming their productivity gains are no more than grocery, then the U.P.C. is creating another $14 billion in net benefits, for a total of

*See Appendix, "17 Billion Reasons to Say Thanks."

about $30 billion benefits. But through our conversations, we believe that the other channels beyond grocery have achieved a lot more soft benefits than grocery has.

So we think the estimate is conservative. The VIC's committee, for example, has taken to U.P.C. enabled processes like cross docking with a vengeance. The actual benefits are much higher outside of grocery. The economic impact of the U.P.C. on the food industry and indeed other retail sectors is easy to characterize. The last twenty-five years have been nothing less than a resounding success. The actual results of this pioneering work is nearly twenty times greater than what was promised in the original business case advanced by the Ad Hoc Committee in 1975.

Today our industry moves more quickly. It does so because the U.P.C. unlocks information. Today the U.P.C. can be directly credited with enabling many of the industries most successful initiatives. Without the U.P.C., there would be no initiatives like Efficient Consumer Response (ECR), specifically, since we have spent the majority of our focus on efficient replenishment. Other areas like continuous replenishment, Vendor Managed Inventory (VMI), Collaborative Planning, Forecasting, and Replenishment (CPFAR), Direct Store Delivery (DSD), to name other important initiatives, which are acronyms not familiar to consumers, but are nevertheless important ones that we are working with today in industry.

In the future, the U.P.C. will continue to reign as the great enabler, as we connect globally through the Internet, as we develop personalized connections across businesses and across geographies. In the future, the U.P.C. will allow different cultures and different peoples to buy and sell products. In the future, the innovation of uniformity will be the key that unlocks information, within and between industries. And in the future, it'll be a smaller world. Can you imagine global trade without the U.P.C.? Dealing with all the conversions from country to country, and language to language. As the Internet and technology tear down geographic barriers, suppliers, retailers and even consumers will become global. There will be no more barriers to getting products to new locations. Product launches will be immediate. Reaching new customers will be seamless.

Today we are also already seeing the future of what a smaller world means. Internet shopping provides everyone with choices and alternatives. Already the number of sites that offer a consumer places and products to buy things are quickly becoming limitless. The U.P.C. is once again the key that will enable a truly global economy. Retailers will have access to new customers, suppliers will have access to new retailers, and customers will have access to everything. None of this would have been enabled without the U.P.C.

In the future there will be new business models. Technology is propelling us into the next century with a multitude of new models. Some will take off, and others won't. Some will provide value to all players and some won't. Companies offering to sell groceries over the Internet surely moves the industry to rethink what business we are in. But could these companies think about doing business over the Internet without the U.P.C.? Offering consumers a choice of 140 categories of national brands, fulfilled at any number of retailers is only possible if a uniform standard code is used to identify all of our products. While the business models of the future are yet to be tested, it's unsure whether the economics are there, unlike with the U.P.C. The very essence of business models rising is predicated on the foundation that we have already established another new business model.

In the future, electronic-based trading, or scan-based trading will use the U.P.C. in certain retail segments to dramatically reduce even the remaining manual effort in stores. Imagine the manufacturers instead of retailers owning inventory in the stores – and wanting to do it. The efficient recounting of inventory received in the stores is completely eliminated, because manufacturers are on the honor system. Even invoices are eliminated because retailers pay manufacturers as U.P.C.s are scanned at checkout. The scan-based trading model isn't new, but it is being rekindled as the accuracy of the U.P.C. scanning has steadily improved, and some recent tests indicate that manufacturers, though skeptical, will also benefit from achieving the illusive revenue growth goal.

So what else is in store? Well, e-commerce will set the pace of how we conduct business. Indeed we've already seem a glimpse of the power with 1998 business to consumer sales just over a billion dollars, and business to business sales of just over a $108 billion. These numbers are only the very modest beginning of what is to come, and it is impossible to imagine retailing online without the U.P.C.

At PricewaterhouseCoopers, our point of view is that soon Electronic Data Interhcange (EDI) communication will be enhanced by two-way interactive dialogue through the Internet between manufacturers and retailers. For example, manufacturers will create portals of communication targeted not just at a customer retail organization, but at the individuals within that organization that need their information – the buyers. The folks at the retail end are laying out the stores getting exactly the information they need about manufactured products as they're completing their job. While there will be varying technologies in the Internet to pass the information back and forth, all of the information passed back and forth contains the U.P.C. The power of intimate communication with the consumer has already begun with data-mining applications. The U.P.C. is once again at the center of the innovation.

Can you imagine targeted marketing or leveraging data from frequent shopper programs without the U.P.C.? Before the U.P.C., there was no frequent shopper data worth having. *Progressive Grocers'* frequent shopper programs used to involve punching stars in cards we carried in our wallets or purses. My mother got a lasting benefit from punching enough stars in her card to get a set of silverware that she's had the lasting benefit of for forty years, setting her table every night with that set of silverware. But the industry got no lasting benefit from those paper cards. It's the frequent shopper data enabled through the U.P.C., which is going to allow us to do the targeted marketing we are interested in.

Last year the Grocery Manufacturers Association (GMA) put together a special task force to better understand data mining. These data analysis tools are used by direct marketers, financial firms, and others to improve the success of doing business by targeting direct mail offers and, as an example, weeding out high-risk loan applicants. Could data mining, the GMA wanted to know, be used to bring manufacturers and retailers together in our industry to better understand and more efficiently market to today's retail consumers?

The task force brought together seven major manufacturers: Anheuser-Busch, Coca-Cola, Kraft Foods, Nabisco, Pillsbury, Proctor and Gamble, and Warner Lambert. Wegman's Food Markets, based in Rochester, New York, offered it's frequent shopper data for analysis. Stripping it of any identifying consumer information that might trigger privacy concerns, but not stripping it of the all-important U.P.C. information. For example, one analysis during the project, tried to find out whether shoppers who were sensitive to one type of U.P.C.'s in a store are similarly sensitive to promotions across all the other categories in the store that they buy. The analysis found that there were a particular group of shoppers that bought certain products because of promotions, but that promotions were not very important in their shopping decisions to buy other products in the store. This small group represented only twenty-five percent of Wegman's annual sales, and could be a target for an innovative method of promotion directly to those consumers, by targeting their frequent shopper data.

We look to the future to even greater rewards of the U.P.C. as it integrates with the EAN standards in 2005. As e-commerce nudges to push information faster and faster, the U.P.C. will play a bigger and bigger role. Now while we'll compare apples and oranges, to give an idea of how big a role the U.P.C. annually plays, well, the $30 billion worth of annual savings is bigger than the market capitalization of one of the market's fastest growing companies, Amazon.com, which has a market cap of only $21 billion compared to the U.P.C.'s benefits. And the accumulated benefit of the U.P.C. is bigger than one of the world's favorite brands – McDonald's – annual sales. While we have said that there are 17 billion reasons why we are here to say thanks, the reality is, we've only just begun.

FROM VISION TO REALITY

BOB L. MARTIN

SINCE THE INTRODUCTION OF THE UNIVERSAL PRODUCT CODE, THE SYMBOLOGY HAS FACILITATED EFFICIENCY IN MULTIPLE INDUSTRIES BY ALLOWING COMPANIES TO EFFECTIVELY MANAGE INVENTORY, AUTOMATE THE ORDERING OF STOCK, AND PROVIDE A FASTER AND MORE ACCURATE CHECKOUT FOR CUSTOMERS. NO COMPANY IS A BETTER EXAMPLE OF USING THE U.P.C. TO IMPROVE ITS BUSINESS THAN WAL-MART.

AS A KEY INDIVIDUAL THAT LED THE DEVELOPMENT AND OPERATION OF ITS TECHNOLOGY CAPABILITIES DURING THE SYMBOL'S FORMATIVE YEARS, BOB MARTIN RECOUNTS HOW THE U.P.C MADE ITS WAY INTO THE RETAIL APPAREL AND NON-FOODS INDUSTRY AFTER YEARS OF GROCERY RETAIL USE, AND THE DRAMATIC IMPACTS IT HAS HAD ON THE BUSINESS OF WAL-MART AND RETAILERS ALL OVER THE WORLD. MR. MARTIN DISCUSSES HOW THE BAR CODE HAS CHANGED THE WAY SUPPLIERS AND MANUFACTURERS WORK WITH ONE ANOTHER AND HOW RETAILERS REACT TO THEIR CONSUMERS. HE SUPPLIES THE SAVINGS FORECAST BY THE RETAIL INDUSTRY AND REPORTS ON THE PROGRESS IN ACHIEVING THEM.

I'd like to dial back the clock just a little bit. June 24, 1986 proved to be the turning point of relations in the retail area between the retailers and the manufacturers. This was when some of the industry leaders (what we called at the time, a bunch of movers and shakers) gathered together in Chicago and decided that they would do some thing to address our perennial issues:

- Long standing adversarial relationships between retailer and manufacturer
- Constant layering in of cost and growing inefficiencies
- Responsiveness to consumer slow and often ineffective
- No clear industry-wide leadership

Hence came the Voluntary Inter-industry Communications Standards (VICS) movement and initiative. The companies represented were in the apparel and department store business. Ultimately it spanned more than just retailers and manufacturers. Many technology people and supplier providers had much to do with what took place.

We were given a mission statement, a direction, and a low budget. Technology was clearly seen as something that was going to be the core, although those of us who were kind of leading the charge were told it was simply an enabler – an enabler to change the rules that drove all those issues that concerned ways to reduce the adversarial relationships between retailer and manufacturer, reduce costs and link closer to the consumer. We were to do things on a critical mass-scale that only an industry standard can provide. This is an oversimplification of the mission statement, but in broad and simple terms it said: take better care of the customer, drive the cost out, fix it, and do it now, we're tired of waiting. The VICS ad hoc efforts were successful enough to so that by 1995 our effort grew to creating voluntary commerce standards and envisaging a day when all retail – globally – would be involved.

The first challenge was to identify a way of standardizing product identification, because so much is driven by product marking. Despite having the credibility of U.P.C. food industry experience to draw on, we did not reach a decision to adopt the U.P.C. easily. In fact it took months for us to get to that point. It was a very wise choice and one that probably moved us ahead a decade faster than had we chosen any other options available at the time. The grocery industry's willingness to support us and the capabilities it provided through the Uniform Code Council drove much of the decision. But more than that. We say that there was more – much more – that could – that was going to happen with standardization of product marking than just speeding up the checkouts and removing the hassle of price checks. The bigger agenda that wanted to be covered, that's what VICS has taken off and done.

In 1995 the VICS became broader than communications – it became the Voluntary Inter-industry Commerce Standards. By 1997, the entire retail pipeline was being covered. Today VICS continues to be a great steward of what's taking place with and on a global basis. By 2000 over 147 member companies, better than about ninety percent of the entire non-food industry volume, were participants.

This has been industry-wide change driven by an ad hoc initiative. The lessons learned from this ad hoc operations were: leadership is vital; professionals with full-time jobs can do the right things for industry; no trade secrets need be given away; members can remain fierce competitors; and the big goal – to seek quantum leap improvements in our operations – can be achieved.

We had fun. History reminds us and it is a familiar lesson that bringing about radical change, setting a new order does not come easily. Machiavelli had it right:

> . . . there is nothing more difficult to take in hand, more perilous to conduct, or more uncertain in its outcome, than to take the lead in introducing a new order of things. Because the innovator has for enemies all those who have done well under the old conditions and lukewarm defenders in those who may do well under the new.

Success did not come easily for the general merchandise sector. There were people clearly behind us; a lot that were going to be along side us if we were successful; and a few that no matter what happened were going to be on the outside. That is just part of the challenge. The mission was to take a hold *across* the industry. Retailers and manufacturers both played a role. They agreed to consider two simple questions – are we going to use U.P.C. and, if so, when?

The Fastest Route Between Two Points

0 22612 01210 3

Is A Straight Line

Universal Product Codes Are Required for All Items
BEFORE ORDERS WILL BE WRITTEN

First Message.

If You Don't Draw The Line

0 22612 01210 3

We Do

Universal Product Codes Are Required for All Items
BEFORE ORDERS WILL BE WRITTEN

Stronger Message.

The first marketing message was pretty positive. It said you're just not going to get a purchase order unless you use U.P.C. coding. When companies did not comply, a little bit stronger message, more than a marketing campaign but still polite was needed. It said if you don't draw the line, then we do, literally. In the case of Wal-Mart, Kmart, and so may others, it became a condition of doing business. Our mandate was to better serve the consumer and to take the industry further.

Manufacturers had spent most of their time taking care of retailers as the customer; and retailers too much time playing at being customers. There was little view, or little communications, or little measurement aimed at the target – the end customer and consumer. Quick Response (QR) is a terminology that has come to stand for the deep and broad equation. This term and others, Vendor Managed Inventory (VMI) and Efficient Consumer Response (ECR), which seems to be the more global phrase, represent the ultimate goal, the real payback, and the real vision that the U.P.C. offered the retailers and manufacturers.

It becomes clear that these little black bars that we're celebrating today are in fact a best friend to the consumer. They have empowered change of so much, not just the conveniences of the shopping experience, but of operations all the way to where value gets driven and how well all consumers can be served today.

Simply stated, regardless of what you call it, the thesis is setting the right product in the right place and doing it more efficiently, more effectively, more competitively, and continuing to seek improvement. The goal for savings that was set out largely by VICS, along with Kurt

Salmon and Associates and others who helped us study the situations was $25 billion. Because of the vast amount of inefficiencies, mainly excess inventory stacked up across every stage in the supply chain, $25 billion in savings was possible by just cutting out the excess inventory, by using common marking techniques, by sharing information, and doing a better job of efficiently getting inventory through the pipeline.

Although the *Lead Time Reduction* graph can't represent all of retail in the general merchandise side, it does represent what it's been for all the proactive companies grouped across merchandise categories, spanning not just apparel, but basic consumer products. The amount of improvement, the reduction in number of days it takes from the time the order is first placed and the product is delivered is shown in the *Improvements to Inventory Levels* graph. The savings in actual dollar bills generated when inventory begins to come out of the pipeline is an apparent sixty to seventy percent, even greater across some product lines and without sacrificing customer satisfaction. These savings cannot be achieved except through the flow of good and accurate product information. The required flow was beginning to be developed and standardized across industry, with both retailers and manufacturers working on implementation.

In the long run the price tag for inefficiency winds up on the selling floor and right on the shelf. It is a truism that "out-of-stocks" is the greatest insult to a customer. A customer goes through all the trouble to go to a store and look for the product on the shelf and it's not there. Owing to the U.P.C., in the last decade alone, we made a greater than sixty-five

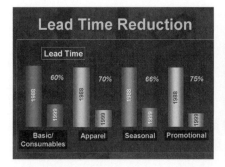

percent reduction in "out-of-stock" situations. What used to be missed sales are now captured. Market share, trust, and brand loyalty all became significant paybacks.

The two graphs below demonstrate the real impact of having an industry-wide standard that allows savings to be generated. In times past retailers mainly tried to push the inventory out of the stores. They displayed what they thought they could sell, or "push" on the customer. It was a little bit more refined than that, but far from a "pull" system in which stores put on the shelves what the customer "told" them they wanted. In truth, the customers pull the item through the store. Operating through the U.P.C. code, means that every time a customer walks out the front door after they crossed the checkout counter they communicated something back. Their message drives replenishment and puts the consumer in control.

When inventory is brought under control store by store and customer by customer, there is a change. It affects how consumers are looked upon, effecting everything from promotional plans to special values offered by a retailer or manufacturer to the basic staple items that are kept on the shelves every day. The U.P.C. code is in fact the agent all the way through the pipeline. Of the $25 billion in potential savings, Kurt Solman Associates studies documented that by the mid-Nineties $13 billion was being saved in the apparel industry alone through inventory control.

The real message, however, is that the consumer won. U.P.C. has done things for the consumer that just simply could not have happened

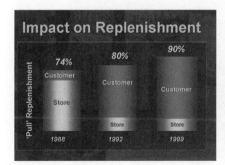
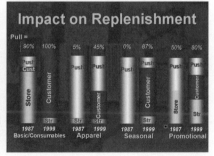

without it. But not only has the consumer won, industry has won, and significantly benefited as well by getting to really understand how to compete in today's environment. Technologies help industries respond to consumers that know more, expect more, and are increasingly more in control.

Going beyond the basic or threshold savings, today one finds oneself in the midst of the new imperative – data sharing. It is a process that affects tailoring how an individual store looks, serving a particular customer's preference, or having the timing right by joining in common planning. Of special note is the serious and widespread work being done in Collaborative Forecasting and Replenishment (CFAR) as it relates to merchandise planning and availability. This and the other new models could not happen without the critical technology that runs the entire pipeline. Information about when the customers shop, and what they buy ties back to what began with the U.P.C., which is now driving the system paradigms between retailers and manufacturers farther than was ever imagined.

A manufacturer using shared data introduces a new product and knows it's accurately marked, gets feedback as to how it's performing, and knows what the customer preferences are. This knowledge produces improvement in the pipeline that benefits the customer and increases profitability. Progress in new items, as the graph shows, is but one example of how business culture has been changed by the technology. The once adversarial relationship has become one of collaboration between players – consumer, retailer, and manufacturer.

My basic message has to be that there is still a long way to go to realize the full potential of even today's technology and systems, not to mention those yet to be developed. A KSA survey done in 1997 indicated 65% of companies having achieved basic implementation. Only 35% had embraced process redefinition with a mere 10% using callabarative practices. The pace has picked up in the succeeding years and the curves point higher.

A study was done sampling seventy-five companies doing about $300 billion worth of industry business and extrapolating to the total industry reports. How did we get all the way from $13 billion out to $102 billion? The $13 billion that came out of soft goods is now viewed by VICS as something more on the order of $54 billion in annual savings potential coming from, among other things, increased sales, increased margins, driven out costs, markdowns that are not taken and, happier customers. Extend the soft goods side savings techniques and its $54 billion benefits to the rest of the store where VICS is now operating, so encompassing all of retail and you pick up another $48 billion with more that $7 billion of that demonstrated as doable.

Technology utilizing U.P.C. has brought us together. It has eliminated emotion, it has presented us with facts, it has given us measurement, it has given us speed, it has given us efficiencies to totally change the way we do business. The underpinning is shared information. And the U.P.C. code has enabled sharing of information throughout the system,

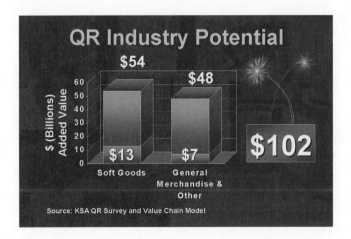

not just at the checkout. The code goes through sales or administrative processes to the payment of the invoice – from in the back door to out the front door. Retailers and manufacturers have been brought together, in a new business model impossible before industry-wide standards. These new technologies and the systems that grow from them are the stuff of competition. For an individual company to ignore them is to invite loss of market share; to embrace and perfect them is the stuff of growth, service to the consumer, and profit for the employee and stockholder.

The Universal Product Code in Perspective: Context for a Revolution

David K. Allison

The Smithsonian Institution's National Museum of American History is dedicated to inspiring a broader understanding of the United States of America and its many people through collecting and preserving more than 17 million artifacts. Dr. David Allison explains what motivated the museum to create an exhibit displaying the story of the Universal Product Code among such other relics as the original Star Spangled Banner and Henry Ford's 1913 Model-T.

Dr. Allison interprets the story behind the U.P.C., how the U.P.C., which is physically small, has become such a giant, intellectually and historically. He compares the bar code with other artifacts featured in the Information Technology and Society Section of the museum and explains why the symbol, its standards formation process and the technological progress of the U.P.C. has such an important place in history.

The historical context for the U.P.C. can be explored from many perspectives. This essay examines how the U.P.C. story fits into the history of computing and communications as presented in the exhibition *Information Age: People, Information and Technology,* a permanent display at the National Museum of American History in Washington, D.C. On the twenty-fifth anniversary celebration of the U.P.C. in 1999, a section on U.P.C. history was added to Information Age. This essay will explore how the display relates to other stories the exhibition presents.

In many ways, the story of the U.P.C begins with Samuel Morse's invention of the telegraph. Figure 1 shows Morse's first experimental model. The transmitter is in the front. It worked when an arm you see moved up and down over the metal "code slugs." As this happened, wires at the end of the arm went in and out of cups of mercury, making and breaking an electrical circuit. This in turn went through an electro-magnet on the receiver, which is in the back of the picture. As the magnet changed, the arm moved and reproduced on a paper tape the same pattern found in the transmitter.

Samuel Morse's vision for the telegraph was expressed in a phrase he penned in his notebook before he began building this first device. Having learned that electricity could pass rapidly through long lengths

Figure 1: Morse's First Experimental Model of the Telegraph.

of wire, he wrote in 1832, "I see no reason why intelligence might not be instantaneously transmitted by electricity to any distance."

Morse envisioned using electricity to provide a means for instantaneous communication, in the form of coded signals that represented "intelligence." In many ways, this initial vision still underlies today's information age – and the story of the U.P.C. in particular. Electromagnetic radiation provides speed of transmission. Intelligence is coded in this form so it can be moved from one place to another. To skip ahead, is it surprising that in 1949, when Joe Woodland began thinking of a code for an automated system for pricing groceries, the first code that came to his mind was Morse's code?

In the case of Morse's telegraph, just as in the case of the U.P.C. over a century later, crafting a device to encode signals was only the beginning of the story. The device was only valuable if it was connected to other devices on a network. Solving network problems, and linking cities across the United States, and later around the world, drastically changed the nature of society.

The humble device that started it all, the telegraph, was a business instrument. Telegraph operators needed special knowledge and training. The device was operated only in a business environment. Almost no one had a telegraph at home, and only few businesses ran their own telegraph offices. In comparison, the telephone marked a major transition. It was a change from instant communication as a service, to instant communication as an individual experience. It was a transition from communicating from station to station to communication from person to person.

Figure 2 shows the experimental telephones of Alexander Graham Bell, which are on display in Information Age. The evolution of the telephone is a complicated story with many chapters. When Alexander Bell invented the telephone in the 1870s, business people of the time believed it to be largely a waste of time. They argued that the most important issue was not creating a new means of communication; it was making the telegraph work more efficiently. Their theory was that for the telephone to be economical, everyone would have to have one. The cost would be phenomenal, and, they postulated, all those telephones would be idle the majority of the time.

We all know how wrong that judgment was. But it did indeed take time and huge capital investments to make the telephone valuable. In

*Figure 2: Alexander Graham Bell's
Experimental Telephones.*

looking back at this transition, a question for today is: Are U.P.C.s, or automated product identification systems, now at the point of moving from a business environment to a general public environment? If so, do the stories of transitions of related technologies in the past offer useful lessons?

Samuel Morse began an electrical communication revolution that brought us telegraph, telephone, wireless, broadcast radio, and ultimately television. During this same period, new technology was also being developed for processing information. Processing is inherently more difficult than communication, because it involves more steps. Data must be input, stored, changed according to sets of rules or procedures, reread, then output in human readable form. Consequently application of electrical and later electronic systems for information processing lagged behind their application to communication.

A major step forward came with the development of punched card machines as seen in Figure 3. The first successful punched card system was developed by Herman Hollerith to process the 1890 census. Hollerith quickly recognized that his system was useful not only to government but also to many areas of business that had to process large quantities of data. Punched card technology provided a foundation for much of the data processing industry. By the 1930s, punched card technology was being applied to processing Social Security Administration data. Indeed, it is hard to conceive how such a program could exist without automated information technology to support it.

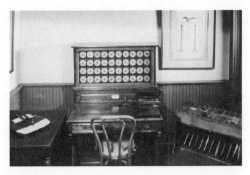

Figure 3: Herman Hollerith's Punch Card System.

What the Morse telegraph was to instantaneous communication, the ENIAC computer was to information processing. The Army created ENIAC during World War II to compute ballistics tables. The name "ENIAC" is an acronym that stands for "Electronic Numerical Integrator and Computer." The machine filled a room 30 feet by 50 feet used 18,000 vacuum tubes, and required huge cooling fans. Figure 4 shows how ENIAC looked in operation. It cost around half a million dollars, a large sum of money for the time.*

Figure 4: The Electronic Numerical Integrator and Computer.

*Pieces of the ENIAC are now spread around the world. The Smithsonian owns most of what is left however, and most of that is on display in Information Age.

ENIAC was unquestionably a turning point for American society. Historians often quibble about whether or not ENIAC was really the "first digital computer." Other forms of automated calculating machines existed before ENIAC, even one that was electronic. There is no debate, however, that ENIAC was the machine that began the computer industry in the United States. Before ENIAC, no one really thought it was possible – or worthwhile – to try to make a business of developing calculating machines that used electronic tubes instead of mechanical wheels and gears to make calculations. The speed that would be gained through electronics was not seen as worth the cost or risk. ENIAC proved that in some cases it was worthwhile, especially when the calculation could be included in "programs" of coordinated, multiple steps. It is interesting to note that in 1949, *Popular Electronics* said that even though ENIAC had 18,000 vacuum tubes and weight 30 tons, computers in the future might have only 1,000 vacuum tubes and weigh only 1.5 tons!

The ENIAC was built to help the Army win World War II. Compared to money spent on calculating devices before World War II, ENIAC was expensive. On the other hand, compared to the development of the Atomic Bomb – the largest technology program of World War II, development of ENIAC was small-time.

As the United States moved from war back to peace, there was little question in anyone's mind that science and technology would be a dominant force that would change the future. Never had scientific research seemed more important. Most people at the time, however, would have said that we were moving into the "Atomic Age," a time when atomic power would not only determine which were the leading nations of the world, but also become the foundation of almost everything we did. Power would become "too cheap to meter," as some said. An "Information Age" was hardly envisioned. At most, experts said, we might have a few dozen computers. After all, they were huge, expensive, likely to break down, and only had special uses for science or government.

Computers became highly integrated with the evolution of the Cold War. The Federal Government was the major supporter of computer development in the early days, and the major customer. This had a major effect on the history of computer technology and how it was used. Imagine for a moment how different computer development would have been had World War II never happened. Would it have developed naturally from the foundation of punched card machines? Would small systems have come first? In any case, the context unquestionably set the pattern for computer development in the 1940s and 1950s. Conversely, imagine what issues there might be today about "global systems" and the Internet if Cold War tensions were similar to those of the 1950s. The point is that historical context is essential in establishing parameters for the path that technology will follow.

The first commercial computers were expensive. For investment in them to be economical, users aimed to maximize the time that the central processor was running. Programs were written externally and sent through the computer in batches. This style of "batch processing" limited the direct relationship between computers and users. "Real-time," or "on-line computing," the form that underlies automated systems, and personal computers today, developed only gradually. A major step, and one that we highlight in Information Age, was the development of Semi-Automatic Ground Environment System (SAGE). Like so much early computer development this was driven by defense requirements, in this case, the need to protect the United States from attack by Soviet bombers armed with nuclear weapons.

The billions of dollars that the Government poured into SAGE helped resolve many of the fundamental aspects of developing real-time computer systems. Among other things, the modem emerged from this effort. So did core memory. SAGE engineers also pioneered many aspects of direct relations between computer users and systems. Instead of using the familiar mouse of today, SAGE operators used a light gun to interact with the workstation (Figure 5).

Figure 5: A SAGE Operator at a Workstation.

SAGE systems remained in operation for many years. Fortunately, they never vectored fighters to a real Soviet bomber that had to be shot down. Their historical importance was in later systems that built on the technical foundation they pioneered. The most direct spin-off was the SABRE airline reservations system. But other real-time transaction systems, such as those used in supermarket automation, would follow.

In 1948, Joe Woodland and a colleague at Drexel University, Bob Silver, began thinking about a system that could be used for automatically recording prices of objects at retail sales counters. Woodland assumed the task of designing the basic scheme for product identification. Woodland actually left his position at Drexel and went to Miami Beach to stay with his grandfather to work intensively on his idea. On the beach one day, he devised the notion that a means of identification should be a set of bars. Because he wanted the symbol to be omnidirectional, he turned the bars into a circle. This idea was refined and developed into the patent application he and Silver filed in 1949.

Woodland's original idea was for a device and not a full system. For automated pricing to become truly valuable to retailers, it would have to be incorporated into a comprehensive system that linked pricing not only to more accurate processing of customer orders, but also to inventory management, distribution, warehousing, and other functions. As SAGE had shown, such wide-ranging systems were now possible with information technology, but they were very expensive and technically demanding. Only sectors like National Defense could afford them. Years of additional technology development had to occur before they would be competitive in the retail sector.

When IBM was unwilling to buy his patent for the price he asked, Woodland sold it to Ford, who later sold it to RCA. The circular symbol he originated would later come back as one of the competitors in the choice for the Universal Product Code.

Retail was not the only economic sector that had to deal with massive growth in the post-World War II era. Another important sector was banking. In many ways, their problems were analogous to what retailers were facing.

Checking accounts had existed before World War II, but after the war, the number of accounts – and the number of checks issued – multiplied rapidly. How were banks to process them all? Computers should provide an answer. In 1950, Bank of America took the lead and approached Stanford Research Institute to provide a system. The requirement was a system that could handle 55,000 transactions per day, with updates to customer accounts, distribution of checks to external banks, and balancing of daily operations. Banking, a capital-intensive industry sector if ever there was one, was capable of handling the huge initial cost. The result was Electronic Recording Machine Accounting (ERMA). Figure 6 shows its main computer.

Banks had a similar problem to retailers. How could they link checks to a computer system? Instead of printed bar codes they used magnetic ink. Since laser readers were not available, it was a practical, but a more expensive solution. General Electric, which built the computers, decided to use transistors rather than tubes in the processing circuits. Doing so required enormous costs, as transistors were just becoming commercially available. But they were absolutely essential for a device that would meet the Bank of America requirements. The components of this system mirror the state of computer and identification technology at the time. The technology was good enough for a central system, but probably still too limited for a distributed system like supermarket scanning. RCA, a player in the U.P.C. development bid, bid on the ERMA project, but lost to G.E. IBM did not bid.

Figure 6: The Electronic Recording Matching
Accounting's Main Computer.

The revolution initiated by supermarket scanning and the Universal Product Code was a revolution that makes sense in context. To be successful, it required the availability of critical core technologies. It required solid-state computer systems that were robust enough to be deployed in stores, laser scanning technology, network technology, storage systems, and specialized software.

This revolution in technology alone was not enough, however. Equally important was a change in how business was conducted – development of standards, new relations between manufacturers and retailers, and innovative business practices.

Underneath it all are human stories, stories of people who took risks and made a difference. The U.P.C. exhibition at the Smithsonian includes an interactive display that lets visitors hear audio clips of some of the leaders of the development of the U.P.C. Joe Woodland, who patented the bar code in 1949, briefly explains how he conceived his idea while on the beach in Miami. He said,

> I carried a beach chair down to the beach and I was thinking about it.
>
> I had already determined that it had to be some kind of sticker on each item with the price on it, in some kind of a code. And the only code that I knew was Morse code. I think I learned Morse code as a Boy Scout so I knew about dots and dashes. So I said, "I could put a line of dots and dashes on there," but the trouble with that is that the checker or somebody would have to orient it to the scanner, because I was thinking of a scanner scanning across a transparent belt and picking up the dots and dashes. So I said, "That isn't going to work." But it has to be a code, so I was thinking of dots and dashes and I stuck my five fingers into the sand. And for whatever reason, I don't know what it was, I drew them to me. And I said, "I have wide lines and narrow lines; it's two dimensional now. That's great! I can scan it!" And that was the birth of bar code, right then and there.

George Laurer, a former IBM engineer, says about his design of what became the final symbol,

The U.P.C. as I designed it was a linear bar code that could be printed in the direction of the printing press movement. This reduced the problems of smearing to an absolute minimum. Space was at a premium. They dictated that the area be no larger than one and a half square inches. It became apparent that the code had to be a self-clocking code. The clock, the timing sequence had to be built into the code itself. It had to have a high degree of checking or redundancy. Another requirement was that the code be read at speeds of at least forty inches per second as the symbol went over the scanner. Also you had to realize the amount of processing was very limited in the '70s. We didn't have the powerful computers that we have today.

Alan Haberman headed the committee charged with selecting a symbol design that could be a reliable standard. He recalls,

The art of creating a standard is to know how somebody is going to use it. The wider the consensus, the more successful it should be. It was necessary for companies all over the world in diverse industries that are normally competitive with each other — manufacturers and buyers — to agree for our symbol to become a standard. And that is what made the Universal Product Code such an unusual thing. Five executives from two different kinds of businesses set up a committee to investigate this — but they kept it open. Everything they did they publicized. They went back and forth to the associations, they hit the newspapers, they went to the government, and they went to the labor union and told them what they were doing. By the time we were ready to announce we had a symbol, the whole world knew what we were working on. They knew that we were going to try to save everybody money and do a better job of service and get the prices right.

So we made our announcement of a selection at a big convention of food merchants in the United States. When we asked for a raise of hands, "Will you guys come along?" The vote was 1,000 percent yes. What we did was pre-sell it on a very wide basis.

Paul McEnroe, who led the development team at IBM that created a full-scale implementation of grocery checkout system based on the U.P.C. remembers,

I was meeting with a senior IBM engineering executive from headquarters and he was down to review our proposal and I had a very rough kind of check stand there. I had clothespins holding some of the things together. We told him what we were going to do about how we were going to read this symbol. We showed him in round numbers what the symbol looked like.

He said, "This is the most ridiculous proposal I've ever seen in my entire life. You're going to run this symbol by this open hole here at 100 inches a second while it's spinning and being carried at varying speeds by a human hand. You're going to read that and you're going to read it on simultaneously fifteen different check stands and go look the price up in the back of the room and come out and print it out before the person is tired waiting to hear the result. You're nuts." But he said, "Hey, you guys have a good reputation, this is a new venture. I'm going to give you funding for a year and I'm not coming back until a year to the day. And if this thing doesn't work your desks are in the parking lot."

He came back a year to the day and we showed him the scanner. He picked up a pack of cigarettes, which had a label on it, and he threw it from one end of the check stand to the other, bouncing along the tabletop. The scanner read it, even though it was spinning while he threw it.

He said, "Well, I'll be doggoned." He actually said something more strong than that. But, in any event, he actually made us take the covers off the bottom of the check stand because he wanted to be sure we didn't have one of the engineers down there keying the right answer in! But it worked.

Finally, Tom Rittenhouse, Chairman of the Uniform Code Council, reflects on what will make the significance of the U.P.C. grow in the coming century,

> The word for the new millennium is "collaboration." We will need collaborative planning and forecasting. What that really means is that a manufacturer and a retailer sit down together and decide what they want to do, set parameters, and then determine how they're going to move forward in areas like co-operative planning of inventory assortments. When all that takes place, the retailer has the opportunity to put the goods consumers want at their disposal at the right time at the right place, without adding additional costs to the supply chain, in fact eliminating costs from the supply chain. That's how, by working together in a non-adversarial relationship, costs can be reduced from the supply chain and value can be added to the consumer.

The perspective of the past is vital to ability of today's visionary practitioners as they continue to encourage collaboration among the participants in the marketplace. Technology will persist in propelling the economic and societal benefits of the U.P.C. ever further as the Internet, e-commerce, and the increase in information networks throughout many areas of business grow in the next twenty-five years.

Standardization: The Philosopher's Stone of the Information Age

Ronald L. Nicol

Industry standards — common technical architectures and specifications that are broadly used in an industry — are like the mythical philosopher's stone, which turned lead into gold. In an industry where industry standards emerge three key changes occur, multiplying value generation in the industry. Consider the PC industry and its standard, the Windows/Intel architecture, as an example. Complimentary products become much more affordable and widely available, i.e., software for MS/DOS PCs. The market is opened to new entrants, increasing supply, and innovation. And prices decline, fostering greater volumes and broader utilization. The PC revolution as we have experienced it could not have happened without the emergence of the Windows/Intel standard.

The process of creating a standard is subtle and complex, but once established, strong standards are hard to change. For example, the four foot eight and one-half inch standard for the width of railroad tracks used in the U.S. has its origins in the design of chariots in ancient Persia 5,000 years ago. Standards are likely to be stronger when sellers control the standard, when the industry ecomomics favor the emergence of a dominant seller ("winner-take-all"), when the rate of innovation is high, when buyers are fragmented, and when the inherent value of interoperability is high. The PC industry has all of these characteristics.

Standards can have a dramatic effect on how companies compete and how they win and lose in the game of strategy. In fact, standards are now taking center stage in some of the battles that are occurring, particularly in the technology sector.

What is a standard? How do we define a standard? How do standards create value? How do companies think about creating value in the marketplace? And I will offer a call for action for those involved in the development of standards.

There is tremendous tension in today's world between creating standards and capturing the values embodied in those standards. The challenge is to know how much value to give away and how much to keep. Companies that can create standards and keep control of them can generate a tremendous amount of market value. One of the best examples is Microsoft, which in the development of Microsoft Windows created an ad hoc standard that nearly everyone uses. In the process, Microsoft was able to capture and keep the value through licensing fees and other means. By contrast, we have standards such as the U.P.C. and TCP/IP, which enable us to communicate in today's world. However, no one really captured the value of these standards; the value has accrued to the public at large, and it has been a tremendous benefit to the world.

The economic view of a standard is that it is a product specification that serves as a common reference point for multiple parties. There are five general types of standards. First, there is the product standard. Examples of this are Microsoft DOS or the IBM PC. These are products where you can actually see the substantiation of a standard, you can copy it, reverse engineer it, and others can make products that look and work similarly to those products. This creates an ad hoc standard.

A second type of standard is a technical standard, which delineates how things should work with the help of technical or engineering specifications. Using communications standards such as TCP/IP and TDMA, for example, our cell phones work across many regions, at least in the United States. Unfortunately, there are no worldwide telecommunications standards so many of us have to carry three or four different phones depending on where we're going in the world.

A third type of standard is process standards, which specify how we are supposed to do things. For example, process standards would lay out how the clinical pathways in medicine claims. In addition, there are performance standards, which prescribe how well something should work. For example, if a product meets a performance standard of ISO 9000, it satisfies a specific set of criteria. And finally, there are format standards, which define how things should look. This would include accounting standards for income statements and balance sheets and also ways of representing things like weights and time.

One of the most significant developments in our economy has been how standards create value. To begin with, we are seeing a dramatic reduction in cost of processing. We're all familiar with Moore's law, which says that the number of transistors on a given area of a chip will double every eighteen months. The result has been cost declines in information processing that are exponential.

At the same time, we're seeing an explosion of bandwidth in telecommunications through technologies such as wavelength division multiplexing and optical switching. Boston Consulting Group (BCG) recently did some benchmarking that shows bandwidth on a given strand of optical fiber is tripling every year. So processing has become a lot cheaper, and moving information is a lot less expensive.

A third development is the network effect: As you start to connect people together, they want to talk with each other; as you add more people to a network, the value goes up as the square of the number of people on the network. For example, with two people on the network, there are two possible combinations. If you add a third person, there are six possible combinations. And if you add a fourth person, there are twelve possible conversations. As more and more people connect, the value of the network goes up dramatically. But this would not work without standards for how people communicate with each other. Having a standard way to communicate – both in the form of language and in the form of technical standards – creates a huge amount of value in the network.

With the development of standards several things happen. Transaction costs go down because it's easier to communicate between businesses, and the value of the organization's communication goes down as well. Once standards are in place, smaller businesses can actually be quite successful, so the size at which a business is viable is going down. Today we see very successful small information-oriented businesses, which take advantage of the standards to achieve competitive positions.

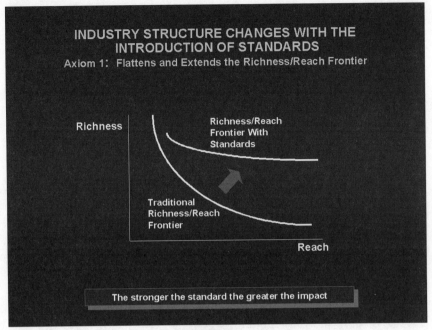

Exhibit 1.

With information there has traditionally been a tradeoff between richness and reach (Exhibit 1). Richness is the amount of information you can transmit through a given channel – in other words, the content. It's easy to provide specific information to a few individuals and to customize that information. But customizing information for large numbers of people has always been a problem. For example, television commercials reach large numbers of people but the information is not customized to individuals.

Standards create the opportunity to redefine the relationship between richness and reach. As people develop more standardized ways to communicate, it's possible to reach more people with less information. Standards also allow you to reduce the amount of asset specificity, which can dramatically affect the economics of an industry (Exhibit 2).

At Ford Motor Company on January 5, 1914. Henry Ford preemptively announced he was going to double the wage rates of all of his hourly workers. At the time, one newspaper on the liberal side, said he was saving the American worker. It said this was great because people were going to be able to buy more goods and services; it was going to

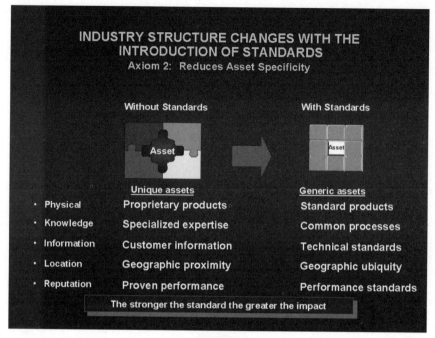

Exhibit 2.

help the economy. Of course, not everyone was so enthusiastic. The *Wall Street Journal* quoted C.E.O.s of the day saying that Henry Ford was destroying American business.

Why did Henry Ford do what he did? Not because he was a great guy who wanted to give away a lot of his profits. In fact, if you understand the challenge he was facing, he had no choice. Employee turnover was about 380 percent at his plants. The reason it was so high was that Ford had developed something no one else knew about: the moving assembly line. The economic advantage that Ford obtained from using interchangeable parts on a moving assembly line gave him tremendous advantage in the marketplace. He could build cars much faster and much more efficiently than any of his competitors could. Unfortunately, Ford workers got bored with tightening lug nuts and nothing else; they wanted to put together whole transmissions across town at the Dodge Brothers, so many of them left. The Ford public relations department put an interesting spin on Henry's announcement. They said that Ford was doubling the wage rate so that more people could afford Ford Model T cars. But we now know that it was more than that.

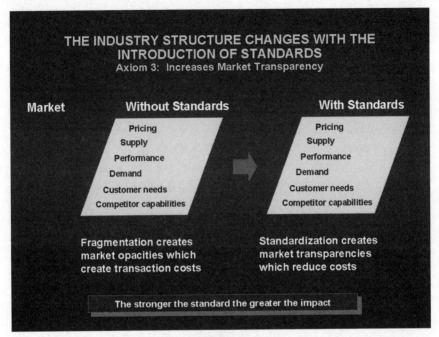

Exhibit 3.

Standards lead to interchangeability of assets, and when this interchangeability is possible, it leads to deconstruction of the industries to the benefit of consumers. The other thing standards do is increase market transparency (Exhibit 3). When you have standards, everyone knows what they are and everyone can make use of them. This eliminates some of the fragmentation in industries, and it also creates more competitive environments. People can compete on pricing, supply, performance, and demand. As standards develop, competitors can carve out a piece of that business and develop it for themselves.

All of these developments lead to a dramatic change in the economics of business. The cumulative effects of the expansion of richness and reach, the effects of reduced asset specificity, and the increase in market transparency lead to much more competitive environments. They can also lead to more value for the end consumer.

The value that accrued from the U.P.C. really ended up in the hands of the customer, and that's the hallmark of a good standard. In the late 1970s, CPM was a very prominent operating system and, arguably, was the emerging standard. When Bill Gates saw the introduction of the

8086 microprocessor, he very quickly bought the company that had developed a rudimentary operating system to run on that chip. This was the beginning of MS-DOS. One of the reasons Windows is not as friendly as it might be is that it still maintained (and still does) backward compatibility to MS-DOS. The same thing is true for Intel's micro-processors. We can still take some of the programs we ran in the early 1980s and put them on a Windows machine. They would still work.

The impact of these factors is evident in the PC marketplace. Because of the backward compatibility and reduced asset specificity, PC prices are lower than they would otherwise be (Exhibit 4). There is more competition and there are better products and services. In addition, there is increasing the market transparency.

The example of the VHS and Beta formats for video cassette recorders provides an interest counterpoint of what can happen if the process of developing standards is not well managed or properly resourced. When VHS and Beta were being developed, Sony's Beta was actually a much better technical standard; Sony had a much better product. Beta was based on a smaller format, more advanced technical

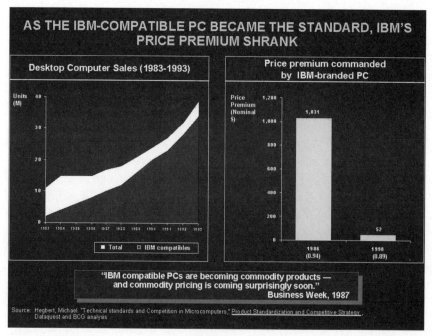

Exhibit 4.

specifications, and it had better resolution. The problem was that Sony wanted to keep too much value, and that strategy backfired. The people who developed VHS seized the opportunity and released the technical specifications of VHS to the open market.

The U.S. railroads during the nineteenth century are an example of how standards emerge. In the mid-1800s, U.S. railroads used a variety of different rail gauges. In 1861, fifty-three percent of the tracks were four feet eight and one-half inches wide, but there were five or six other track widths in use (Exhibit 5). If you were moving goods from Boston to California, you had to go through any number of "transitions" where you needed to move cargo from one train to another. Towns popped up where the transitions occurred, and many jobs were linked to making the transitions. There was a hot debate over the pros and cons of choosing a standard.

The simple solution would have been mandating a track size for the U.S., and that's eventually what happened. But until that was decided, people came up with some rather innovative solutions. One solution involved sliding axles on railcars, which allowed for the adjustment of

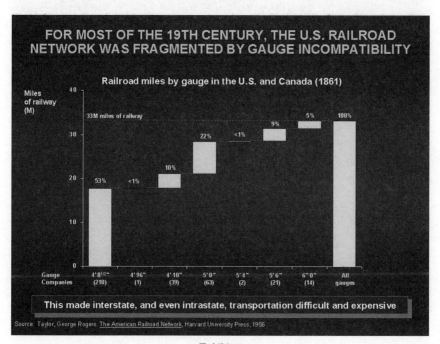

Exhibit 5.

the wheels when the track gauge changed. Another solution involved car hoists, which allowed you to move the cars much more efficiently. And lastly, there was the third rail, which permitted combinations of different track gauges. The problem with this last solution was that you couldn't put enough rails on the system to match all the track gauges in use across the country. Someone actually developed a superior technology based on tracks that were three feet six inches wide (Exhibit 6). It offered better turning capabilities so trains could make sharper turns, and this promised lower costs, but the four foot eight and one-half inch track won out.

There were really two events that brought a standard track gauge in the U.S. First, the Civil War led people to realize how important it was for national defense to be able to move cargo and people across the country. Secondly, when the government commissioned the Pacific Railroad it mandated four foot eight and one-half inch track, and that provided the push that established its dominance.

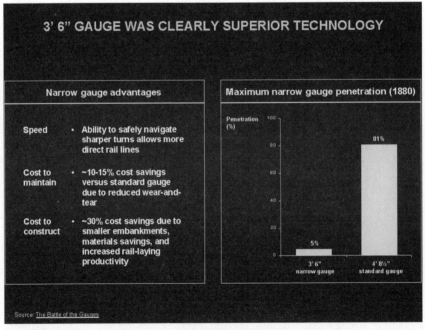

Exhibit 6.

While acknowledging the roles that governments and major events can play in the creation of standards, it is also important to recognize that the establishment of standards is not accidental but a managed process. The railroad case shows the economic impact of standards can be quite compelling. After track gauges became standardized, the cost per mile of rail transportation fell by twenty-five percent (Exhibit 7). However, once it was no longer necessary to move cargo from train to another, people lost jobs.

When we step back and look at standards and what impacts their development, there are a couple of factors that determine whether it will be a relatively weak standard or a relatively strong standard. Typically, a standard set by sellers ends up weaker, to the point that eventually buyers will set the standard. Also, where there are not network effects, there's relatively less force to create a strong standard. When network effects do exist as the standard is getting developed, the value of the standard goes up quite dramatically. And in markets where the rate of innovation is

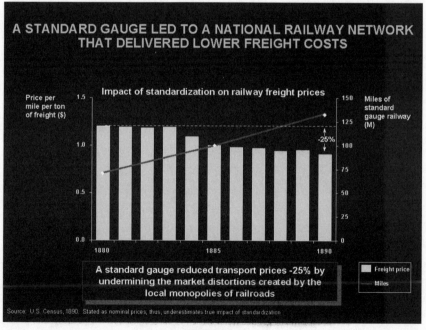

Exhibit 7.

relatively slow, the development of standards becomes relatively weak. By contrast, in fast-changing environments such as today's technology businesses, there's a tremendous focus on standards. And then, of course, there is the degree of fragmentation in the industry. In a highly consolidated industry the weak standards will form because fewer companies will control the standard process or at least parts of it. However, if the industry is fragmented, a standard can be quite strong. Finally, there is the question of interoperability. Where there is not much need for interoperability, strong standards do not develop. Where we see a lot of interoperability, we see very strong standards. The goal in many industries today is to try to find ways to capture standards for their own industry's benefit.

This raises an interesting paradox. In the past, companies such as Microsoft were able to create standards by developing products like Microsoft Windows. Now that everyone sees that this can be done, it's much harder to establish a standard. In fact, once people see a standard emerging they often take steps to stop it. An example that speaks to this issue involves Quicken. With Quicken, Intuit had the dominant franchise for financial software on the personal computer. Intuit then tried to capture the on-line banking business by pulling in a lot of financial institutions as partners. Unfortunately, the banks saw what was happening and hit the brakes. And that's why we don't see as many partnerships with companies like Intuit's. Instead, standards like OFX have emerged that basically put Quicken and its rival, Microsoft Money, on the same footing.

Thinking about the standards-creation process is extremely important, and it depends closely on industry politics. Two things that drive them are represented on a two by two matrix (Exhibit 8). One of them asks who controls the standard? Is the control proprietary or is it open? Is it something that is owned by a particular company or group of companies, or is it something that is open to the industry? The second dimension looks at how the standard is introduced. Is it introduced in a non-cooperative fashion, or is it introduced cooperatively? Businesses would like to be in the upper left-hand corner of the matrix: with proprietary standards that are introduced non-cooperatively. This is where the value is captured. The movement now is to the bottom left box, an open standard, which is not necessarily introduced cooperatively. An example

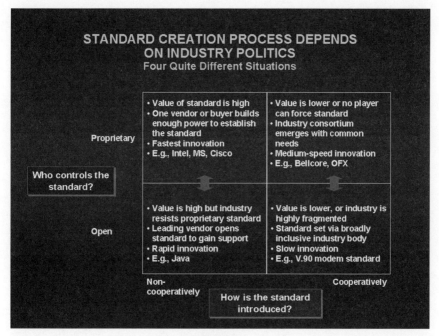

Exhibit 8.

of an open standard is Java. Sun Microsystems realized that it really didn't have the capability to create a standard that it controlled, so it opened Java to the marketplace and released the specifications An interesting battle then developed over Java between Microsoft and Sun; each trying to promote its own flavor so as to appear to be in the lower left hand box while actually having a foot in the upper left hand box.

As things move increasingly to the Worldwide Web, and there is more and more standardization, and as people use interchangeable software modules, it's very difficult for companies such as Microsoft to be able to set standards and control them. There is constant movement. The pressure from the market is to move to the right and down, which are open standards that are developed cooperatively. In fact, this is what happened with modems a few years ago. People determined that they could increase the throughput of a dial-up modem from 33.6 kilobytes to 56 kilobytes. But two groups developed competing standards for 56K communications. There was 3Com's X2 technology facing off against an approach promoted by Rockwell, Motorola, and others. Eventually, the two sides worked out a compromise: the V90 standard.

Standards that have the highest value for consumers are represented in the upper right hand quarter of the matrix. These standards can be managed cooperatively for the benefit of users. A good example of this was Bellcore and the regional Bell operating companies. When AT&T was split up back in the 1980s, Bellcore developed the standards for interoperability in telecommunications. The seven regional operating companies, which were now competitors, supported standards, and Bellcore had to make sure that the specifications were clearly written. The result was the ability to interconnect switches, routers, and many other things in the telecommunications network, which is one of the main reasons why we are now seeing competition in the U.S. telecommunications backbone. Standards make it possible for new wholesale players such as Williams, Qwest, and Level 3 to offer network capacity at costs that are substantially lower than those of incumbents. This value will eventually accrue to the marketplace; we're already seeing it in declining long-distance rates.

Both government and industry need to play important roles in creating a better process for developing standards. Without better processes, companies will attempt to create standards on their own as a means of gaining market advantage. Standards promoters need to step back and think about the environment in which they are trying to create a standard. Does the industry need a weak standard or a strong standard? Should it be developed in a cooperative fashion or in a non-cooperative fashion? If the current standard is weak, perhaps there is not really a compelling need to have a strong standard. In that case, it may make sense for the standard to be developed cooperatively and shaped by the market mechanisms that already exist. On the other hand, if there is a need for a strong standard, then it's important to determine whether it should be created cooperatively or non-cooperatively. It's important to recognize that there are different positions that different companies hold in the marketplace and that particular companies or sets of companies can actually move standards forward more quickly some ways than other ways.

Based on what we know about standards development, once companies achieve market penetration of thirty to forty percent, the standard at that point usually wins. However, it's not just about market share. It's also about trajectory – how rapidly a potential standard gains accep-

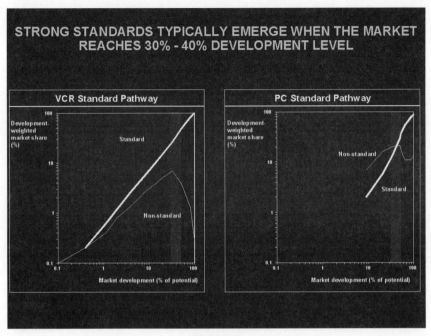

Exhibit 9.

tance. For example, let's look at what happened with VCRs (Exhibit 9). When the VHS standard takes off, the competing, non-standard BETA technology dies. We can apply the same kind of analysis to the battle over PC standards during the 1980s. The IBM PC (standard) and the Macintosh (non-standard) were both good products – the Macintosh was arguably better in terms of engineering and user interface. But Apple tried to hold on to the specifications and the technology; IBM didn't. The result was that PCs became both less costly and less asset-specific. The IBM clone market developed. The rest is history.

When you draw technology adoption curves linearly, you see a very clear S curve. The reason for this S curve is that when a new technology is developed, the probability that people will adopt the technology is a function of two things: how many people have already adopted it and how many people are left to adopt it. And so we have a lemming effect. Consider the case of the Palm Pilot. Initially, there were a few early adopters who bought Palm Pilots even though they sold for more than $200. Nobody really knew if the product would work or what its value would be. But once the first group bought it, others followed on the theory that if it works for Joe, it'll work for me. Then the adoption rate took off to the point where there are fewer and fewer people who don't own Palm Pilots.

There are some important lessons to draw from these experiences. The first lesson relates to market share. Standards tend to come together when the adoption rate reaches about thirty to forty percent. The second lesson relates to speed. Once the standard begins to develop, it occurs very rapidly, and it becomes difficult to manage. And when you reach this point, it's not unlike a reactor going critical: The critical mass happens quite quickly, and the reaction occurs quite fast. What's important is not just the absolute market share but the trajectory of growth. A technology that's gaining acceptance very quickly has a better chance of becoming the standard than one that has a bigger market share but is growing at a slower rate.

In the development of standards it's important to think about the concept of sharing the pain (Exhibit 10). As standards develop, it helps to have everyone involved feel the pain of having to give up value. The goal in standards development is to have everybody give up value at rel-

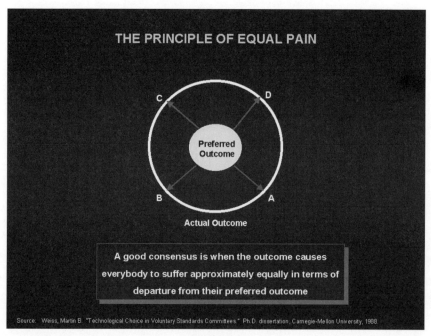

Exhibit 10.

atively the same rate. Collectively, companies end up giving up a lot of value, but the overall market will gain a tremendous amount. If you try to have a particular set of companies absorb a lot of pain without distributing it equally, it will be very difficult to get agreement or to reach an optimal solution.

Looking at a number of case studies and having interviewed many people about how they feel about the way standards are developed today, one of the themes that emerges is that standards are developed at too low a level. As the stalemate over standards increases, it's going to be extremely important to raise the visibility of standards in organizations and to make standards development a priority. If we look at the overall value of standards – and the U.P.C. is a great example – they have the potential to provide a tremendous social benefit. The problem is that it often takes many years for the benefits to materialize. To create competitive markets we need to find the will and the resources to support standards development.

As the world moves more and more to Internet time, it's important to consider what this accelerated pace will mean to the development of standards. Already we have a situation in mobile telephone technology where the standards in Europe and Asia are further developed than standards in the U.S. One thing that needs to happen is there needs to be a way to prioritize the objectives for the standards and how many we need. Clearly, we don't need to have a standard for everything. But we need them where the collective benefit is much larger than the individual benefit.

In many U.S. industries, we are facing a stalemate. We need to establish a process for developing standards that improves overall competitiveness. A vital part of the process is making the case for value. As the record of the U.P.C. demonstrates, there can be huge benefits, and the end beneficiaries are the consumers. We also need to deploy resources in line with the value. For example, if the opportunity once the standard is established is worth $15 billion, then it makes sense to fund standards development at the same ratio that a company might use for any other investment project of that size. The process also needs to address the importance of speed. There is a need for fairly fast deliverables; time must be allowed for adequate input but, the process can't go on indefinitely. Standards bodies and standards development processes tend to get caught up in extreme amounts of detail and minutia. This is why prioritization is so critical. Finally, you need to be able to drive negotiations to a close.

Left to its own devices, the marketplace tends to develop sub-optimal standards. We've seen this in rail gauge technology, PC standards, VCR standards, and many other technologies. In light of all this experience, it probably makes sense for standards bodies to aim for standards that are sub-optimal. What you end up with may not be as good as the best possible standard. But hopefully it will be significantly better than what the market might evolve to on its own.

PANEL DISCUSSION*

LAWRENCE C. RUSSELL, MODERATOR

THE DEVELOPMENT OF THE UNIVERSAL PRODUCT CODE IS A STORY THAT OFFERS IMPORTANT LESSONS IN TODAY'S BUSINESS WORLD. BEHIND THE U.P.C. IS AN ACCOUNT OF A GROUP OF GROCERY INDUSTRY EXECUTIVES WHO PUT ASIDE THE PROPRIETARY GOALS OF THEIR SPECIFIC COMPANIES AND VOLUNTARILY COOPERATED TO REDUCE COSTS ACROSS THEIR INDUSTRY WHILE GIVING NO COMPETITIVE ADVANTAGE TO ANY ONE ENTITY.

THE DISCUSSION OF THE PANELIST REVEALS THE IMPORTANCE OF SUCH AN INDUSTRY MOVEMENT AND HOW IT CAN BE APPLIED TO BUSINESS TODAY. THE PANEL MEMBERS EXCHANGE IDEAS AND OPINIONS ABOUT THE ROLE OF STANDARDS IN THE FUTURE, THE CHALLENGES OF BUSINESS-TO-BUSINESS TRADE OVER THE INTERNET AND HOW TECHNOLOGY WILL REVOLUTIONIZE THE RELATIONSHIP BETWEEN RETAILERS AND CONSUMERS.

*The discussion is reproduced here verbatim in the hope that the reader will be better able to enjoy the feeling of the event. Where editorial clarifiation is needed, it is enclosed in brackets.

Lawrence C. Russell: Before we get started with this part of the program, I would like to recognize some of the people that didn't show up on the program or on any of the videos – they haven't received the recognition they deserve. These people were critical in the development of the U.P.C. There is a risk I'll leave somebody out, but with that caveat, would each of you please stand up as I call your name. Fran Beck – Fran was one of the early designers of the RCA system, which was the first operating system to my knowledge. He is a terrific visionary and engineer and a critical contributor to the U.P.C. effort.

Fritz Biermeier served with distinction on the symbol committee. There were three or four of us that dug into the details of the scanning technology. Fritz always had a penetrating question for each of the submitting companies. He was instrumental in framing the final decision.

Steve Brown, our lawyer and now our historian. He was more than our lawyer – he was our conscious and our supporter when the times got rough.

Murray Eden – Murray was the high-tech visionary from MIT that helped us select a symbol that would endure the inevitable rush of technology that lay ahead. As we look back over the most prolific twenty-five years of technology development in the history of the world and recognize that the U.P.C. symbology technology endures, I guess you can say the decision was a good one.

Barry Franz from Proctor and Gamble – another symbol committee leader, thought leader, interrogator, and decision maker. He contributed significantly to the decision.

Alan Haberman is here. He is getting official recognition, but I want you to know if it were not for Alan's commitment, drive, and ability to maneuver the committee through a number of really tricky situations we would not have the U.P.C. today.

Tim Hammons is here, I think representing Food Market Institute. In my view Tim is actually here representing two people, he and Clancy Adamy, one of the great people in this industry and one of several that had the vision to initiate the entire process. So Tim and Clancy, our hats are off to you.

George Koch – George ran the GMA with distinction for a significant time and he was one of the several industry leaders that initiated the Ad Hoc Committee and the entire process. It was he, Clancy and Mike

O'Conner that got it started. Were it not for those three guys we wouldn't have a U.P.C. today.

George Lauer, IBM, now retired, was one of the great contributors. He helped us see not only the technology, but also how to operationalize the process.

Marvin Mann as the key IBM leader who galvanized the global resources of IBM and worked diligently and patiently with both the Code and Symbol Committees to achieve a viable solution that accommodated the diverse needs of everyone. Marvin Mann is the guy that galvanized the IBM Corporation and made it happen. He recently retired as C.E.O. of Lexmark – one of the great technology success stories of the 1990s. You're going to hear from him tonight. Were it not for Marvin, you would not have this symbol today.

Paul McEnroe was another key member of the IBM team that brought realistic and practical solutions to the many challenges we faced. I understand he's retired now. I can't believe everyone I'm meeting is retired except me.

Michael O'Connor, one of the three people that made it happen. In fact, he was the first person to recognize the critical need for a standard code and symbol because the cost of applying the symbol at store level was prohibitive and the industry couldn't afford to have a multiplicity of symbols in use. He had the foresight to get the other leaders interested, to raise some money, and get the project started. I had the distinct honor – Mike you may recall – after three months of this project, circa 1970, to advise you that we spent that money, and realized that the total effort would take several years. We kept going because we knew it was right for the industry.

Eric Waldbaum – at the time Chairman and C.E.O. of Greenbelt Consumer Cooperative. He was also on the symbol committee. He was, and is, a great thinker, and a great contributor to this effort. Hats off to him.

Joe Woodland an original inventor and major contributor. Joe was with us the whole time. He also had the wisdom to see the operational needs of the technology. I must say that Joe really went out of his way to help us think it through and get it right.

Now a couple of people I want to recognize who aren't going to be with us. Reilly Daniels from RCA, who opened the doors and made all of the development activity, and all of the numbers available to the committee so that we could consider the RCA solution. Reilly recently passed away. Matti Matamore, C.E.O. of Selling Areas Marketing Inc (SAMI). Were it not for SAMI we would not have been able to size [accurately estimate] the cost to the industry of printing the symbol on the vast number of consumer containers in distribution. Matti made all the important information available so that we could understand truly what the economics were. I could go on; I'm sure I'm missing someone. I wanted all of you to recognize those people because they contributed so much to the success.

And now, our distinguished panel. First, we have David Carlson, president, and chief executive officer of Sagence Systems, also known for his vast contributions to the development of the U.P.C. and the Uniform Code Council. As a multi-term governor for the UCC in both the Eighties and Nineties, he has been instrumental in guiding the organization's development and expansion. He brings to the panel his hands-on knowledge as well as his wealth of experiences as senior vice president and chief technologies officer for Ingram Micro and as the past president of Customer Focus Technology and as a former vice president of technology for FTD and before that, Kmart Corporation. Please welcome David Carlson.

Our second panelist is Craig Schnuck, one of the great leaders of the industry today. He's the immediate past president and chairman of the board of the Uniform Code Council. Under his watch, the first joint meeting of the EAN management board, and the UCC Board of Governors was called to order in Chicago, and a new era of global commerce was launched. Craig joins us today as chairman and chief executive officer of Schnuck Markets Inc., a position he literally worked his way up to from a bagger in primary store operations. And today, his company operates more than ninety state-of-the-art markets in Missouri, Illinois, and Indiana. And I must say, I remember this company was one of the great institutions in terms of leadership and innovation many years ago and obviously has continued to do it under Craig's leadership. Please welcome him.

Ted Rybeck, Ted has an extensive list of credits, honors, and awards including the prestigious Kittredge Award, for an analysis of the relationship between technology in an organization, and ROI. Wherever he goes, he is best known for his efforts at spearheading Wal-Mart's successful Internet based collaboration strategy with its trading partners. A strategy that evolved into the first major standard for business-to-business electronic commerce. Ted is the founder and chairman of Surgency [formerly Benchmarking Partners], an innovator of methodologies for demand and supply chain information systems. He teaches at the Massachusetts Institute of Technology and writes extensively on demand and supply chain strategies. Please welcome Ted to our panel.

And then there's Alan Haberman, my dear friend Alan.

Lawrence C. Russell: I could go on for a long time about our professional and our personal relationship. He is our final panelist. His perspective is unique and available to these proceedings. He's been integral to this whole thing from the beginning, and he's stayed with it. I asked him last night, why is he staying with it? Why is he doing this? But he said he loves it, and he's enjoying it. The only governor to have continuously served on the board since 1973, first as a representative of the National Association of Food Chains, then as a public governor, and now as a manufacturer-at-large governor. As a member of the Ad Hoc Committee on Uniform Grocery Product Identification Code and Chairman of the Symbol Selection Committee – and by the way, there was an Ad Hoc Committee, and two subcommittees, namely the Symbol Subcommittee and the Code Subcommittee. Alan was both on the Ad Hoc Committee and Chairman of the Symbol Selection Committee. He has both witnessed and shaped history. He serves as chairman of the ISO/IEC Joint Technical Committee, Subcommittee 31 on automatic identification and data capture. Ladies and gentleman, the chairman of today's event, festivities and a true original leader – Alan. Now I think that some of our panelists have comments and thoughts, so, I'd like to turn it over to the panelists.

Dave Carlson: I'll start. I was a little disappointed that you didn't mention that I chair a group I call the SEMIHF. It's a new California standards group. Those of you who know me, know I grew up in the Midwest. You would appreciate the freedom I found in moving to California. The SEMIHF stands for the Standard Error Messages In

Haiku Form. You know that one of the problems with computers is that error messages are often impossible to understand, like "field VC113 error." Well, we focused on disks and processors, and let me share with you the first two SEMIHF standards:

> Three things are certain,
> death, taxes, and lost data.
> Guess which has occured.
> and
> Your processor failed.
> I am the blue screen of death.
> No one hears your screams.

The other comment I want to make is to acknowledge a battle I've been losing for twenty-five years, and unfortunately, today reminded me again of how big that loss is. This industry for this whole period of time has been using two phrases to talk about benefits – hard benefits and soft benefits. No C.F.O. worth his copy of *How the Grinch Stole Christmas,* would ever put "hard" cash against "soft benefits. Therefore, the investment in "hard" benefits from using accurate and timely information to make better decisions has basically been unexplored in this industry. I hope in the next twenty-five years, somebody will be using a phrase like HPTBD – Higher Profits Through Better Decisions. Thank you.

Craig Schnuck: Tough act to follow here Dave. I've just got a couple general comments on just rehearing the story about how this has happened. It was a very rewarding experience for all of us, and one that we can all learn from and continue to make progress as we go forward. But the other part that I think we have to be conscious of is how rapidly technologies are changing right now, and how important it's going to be for the UCC and all those involved with the UCC to find as many ways as possible to stay up with the rapidly changing technologies and to make sure the standards are developed on a timely basis to adjust to whatever those technological changes might be. And that's far and away, I think, the biggest challenge we have on an ongoing basis with the UCC.

Ted Rybeck: I'm excited about the next anniversary session in twenty-
five years. Alan and I have already worked out the agenda.
That's my focus, but first: It's an honor to be here along all these pioneers. No one has more respect for what's been done over the last
twenty- five years than I do. I've really been an apprentice of Alan's and
a number of folks I've had the good fortune of being able to work with
at the UCC. And the passion I've got is for what happens in the next
paradigm.

You mentioned I teach a C.E.O. course on value chain networking
at MIT. I'm a student there as well of one of the other professors,
Thomas S. Kuhn who wrote a book, *The Structure of Scientific Revolutions*.
It's a fabulous book that tracks about how the way advances actually
happen is not steady progress in the free market of ideas. It goes back to
some of the things David talked about with the history here earlier,
which is, there is a new paradigm and folks spend the next generation or
several generations just filtering all of reality into that paradigm. And I
feel that the pioneers in this room created that paradigm, and that's what
we've done for the past twenty-five years. The disciplines that have come
out of that are invaluable for where we go from here on.

There's been a new paradigm created with the Internet, not just as
technologies, but as a business model itself. The market capitalization
that we've talked about for Amazon and others reflect that. We've
worked with a lot of the venture capital firms that are having extraordinary market capitalization associated with what they're doing. We could
go two ways. We could say, as in conversations with the UCC, "You
know that Internet is really a big sucking sound on Wall Street." And
that's an approach we could take, or we could say, "That could be true
and we empathize with what may be looked on as irrational exuberance
in the future." But there is a fundamental change that has occurred, and
the disciplines that the UCC has developed over the last twenty-five
years need to be applied in this new Internet model in both the B to C
(Business to Consumer) and the B to B (Business to Business) space.

The new paradigm people are hungry for that right now, hungry
for that discipline. However, they don't know where to get it. Most of the
venture capitalists are in the same position. I just came from speaking at
one of the big e-procurement vendor sessions on the West Coast called

Ariba. You may not ever have heard of it, but they just went public after three years and have a market cap (italization) of $4 billion. They do not have a long list of customers but they also brought behind that the buying power of $300 billion of suppliers and consumers. All of a sudden, this clicks and mortar economy is being promulgated.

And they have never heard of the UCC

So what do we do to turn that around? That's one of the things I'd love to learn from the panel. I know Dave's done a lot of work on it and a lot of folks in this room are wrestling with that question. I really do think they need the value of the UCC and don't even know it. So the question become, whose responsibility is that to fix? And if they don't know about it, will they actually build their own capabilities that will eclipse the UCC but without the rigor the UCC brought to it? I actually would look to Al and others to answer those questions.

Alan L. Haberman: I don't know where to begin. Sitting on a platform with Craig is continuity for me. His dad and his uncle were so instrumental in the way we thought and the way we acted. They added so much class to the situation.

The answer to your question, Ted, is Craig. The answer to your question is Tom Rittenhouse, UCC's President. They're a whole new generation, and they're willing to look, they're willing to try, they're willing to experiment. They recognize the speed at which this thing is happening, and they will find some answers. The important thing is they are an open group. They are willing to listen to everyone and everything. The UCC has been going through a gigantic explosion of personnel and has concentrated on training and creating an atmosphere amenable to change and speed. They're reaching a conclusion where they are close to being fully staffed, and I think you're going to see a UCC that's not bureaucratic, that sets its people on a path that is in the tradition of retailing that Tom comes from. You put a bureaucrat in a retail operation and you're dead! This is a young, aggressive, forward thinking and looking team. I look for them to attack the very real, confusing but powerful opportunities of the future.

There's another dimension to the problem that concerns me. It is not just the oncoming Internet. As we heard from BCG [Boston Consulting Group], standards are being made in all areas, by formal and informal consortia, and they're being made all over the world. The UCC recognized a few years back, that they had to participate in the organizations that Larry and I and Tom Wilson and Eric Waldbaum and the boys ducked – we wanted nothing to do with ANSI [American National Standards Institute] and wanted nothing to do with the European standards organizations. But we recognize at this point we are global. We have got to preempt these activities. We've got to be a part of them. And the UCC has jumped into it with both feet.

What bothers me is that the UCC has jumped, and U.S. industry is sitting on its butt. As an expense saving, U.S. industry is currently cutting back on the people in their standards efforts. They are letting CEN, the European standards organization and MITI [Those in charge of the technical standard in Japan] lead the way. Our government has stepped back. NIST has no more money; ANSI is broke – that's a strange way to get work done. I'm concerned. We have a message that I'd like to deliver to U.S. industry – you cannot avoid the international standards setting arena! It's one world. It's one globe. Oh yes, the tremendous ingenuity and technical know-how that America has, wins many times; but we also lose, often simply because we do not support, do not work our will within the international standards operations.

One last thing – and I know I take too long. One possible extrapolation from the PricewaterhouseCoopers *[See appendix.]* study puts meaning to everything that we have done. It updated the costs and returns that we'd assumed in '70, '71, '72 to 1998 dollars and compared them to today's experience – and it's an awfully good job they did. On a rough basis, they calculate that approximately 2.68 percent of retail sales were saved – hard savings and a small component of soft savings. What makes everything that we have done meaningful, gives us the courage to go ahead, is that the grocery industry is still earning the same 1 percent to 1.25 percent on sales. 1.5 percent of sales have been contributed back to the consumer through lower prices, greater variety, more services to continue the decreases in the money consumers spend on food as a proportion of total budget. That's something to be very, very, very proud of. That's something to set as a continuing objective. If this world is going to be an e-business world, or an e-consumer world, UCC has got to be a part of it. And so Tom has already got UCC reaching out in many areas among which is the giant, multimillion dollar project building an extranet capable of handling the entire global distribution channel. There are lots of adventures coming for the UCC. Watch it – it is going to be a great show!

Lawrence C. Russell: I agree . . .

Alan L. Haberman: I dare you to disagree

Lawrence C. Russell: . . . .and I think that it has just begun. I can share with you just a couple points and then will get on to other discussions with the panel.

Point one: The price per unit of computer processing power continues to decline at about twenty-five percent per year. We do not see that changing in our lifetime. Yes, the technologies will change, the production methods will change, but it looks like that's where we're headed. Now, just to put that into perspective for you, if Mercedes had done as good a job since the early 1960s, you'd be able to buy a Mercedes today for one penny. And in a few days, you will hear about the next architecture in enterprise servers. You'll hear about a computer that can simultaneously operate different and incompatible operating systems exchanging data at internal transmission speeds. This machine is capable of processing power in excess of any known requirement. It can incorporate up to thirty-two Intel processors and dynamically partition itself as required by the processing load. The use in WinTel technology means the equipment will be much cheaper than proprietary operating system enterprise servers will. And that's just the beginning. We're in the midst of revolutionary changes in the world of computing power.

Point two: Voice and data transmission capacity is increasing faster than most people appreciate and the cost per unit of information is declining at a similar rate. Over the last three to five years, the speed of telecommunication has increased sevenfold. Within the next two to three years, we will foresee a twenty-fold increase. This increase in "bandwidth" will surely revolutionize our world. Concurrently, cost is declining at a significant rate in communication as it is in computers. Just to make it easy to appreciate the cost for a three minute call from London to New York over the last seven or eight years has declined by two orders of magnitude. You can expect similar reductions in the next decade.

Point three: embedded computer processors will radically change how we live, how we use everyday things like grocery items, appliances, and even our clothes. Did you know that there are six billion computers that are embedded in devices that serve us every day such as toasters, refrigerators and automobiles? You know that there's more computing power today in a sophisticated automobile than there was in a Cray computer fifteen years ago. There's six billion addressable computers today. And most of the new generation of computers will have the same capacity. Within a matter of a few years, we're going to be able to produce processor chips that cost a penny. You will be able to place a processor chip in a can of beans and figure out where it is. That's coming, and it's coming at an incredible rate.

Point four: Intelligent agents – computer programs that search out information that you want or should want will become ubiquitous. Browsers will evolve to intelligent agents that reach out and get information that you want but you don't know that you want. The power of agents in artificial intelligence is moving at a rate beyond belief, and its going to change the way we live, learn, work, and play.

Point five: We are demanding more specific features in everything we buy – more specificity, much more will follow. Did you know that in Japan, you can buy a seven-door refrigerator, and you can specify which side of each door the hinge goes on, and you can specify the color if you are willing to wait two weeks? Did you know that you could buy a high-speed bicycle, a high-performance bicycle, and specify virtually every design characteristic? P.S.: the permutations and combinations of the bicycle number about 300,000. Did you know that Levi today sells jeans and for an extra $10, they will design them for your own body? How about Dell, which produces computers on demand? You specify it, they produce it, and they ship it to you. Did you read the newspaper the other day, where Ford has done a deal with Microsoft to facilitate purchase of a car over the Internet with every detail specified by the consumer? I bet they will collaborate to create a central parts company to make it easier to repair cars. They configure the car and ship it through a dealer. Now I would suggest to you that the demand fragmentation that we are seeing is one of the most fundamental demographic changes in this country and in the developed world.

Point six: Countries and regulatory agencies are struggling to keep up with the rate of change and are invoking change in terms of new regulation and deregulation. We don't have to say anything about telecom, right? Regulation and deregulation – and it's not the same here as it is in Eastern Europe and in Asia. The regulation and deregulation and mergers and alliance partnerships are going to change the very nature of telecommunications. Think in terms of voice over data. It's coming and it's coming within a matter of months. We're going to be having conversations across the Internet and simultaneously shipping data at rates of speed that are today, incomprehensible. I don't have to say anything about the financial industry being regulated, deregulated, merging and changing, restructuring itself. How about the airline industry? How about the trucking industry? So in the three dimensions I would suggest to you, in technology, and demand and in regulation and deregulation, all changing at different rates at different ways throughout the world, it's not surprising that the Internet, in just four years, has gone to 800 million subscribers and over 450,000 businesses doing commercial business on the Internet.

At Unisys we've done taxonomy on those 450,000 companies and found that there are twenty-one different ways that people are making money and a fair number of ways to lose money also. Unfortunately twenty of the twenty-one undermine the profit-making structure of the non-Internet companies that are engaged in commerce today. Twenty out of twenty-one, in effect, undermine the profit structure of the "old economy." Asia.com has just came alive. Its actually called China.com but the real name is Asia.com. It's a portal to half the world's population. Just coming alive. Did you know that 25 percent of the revenue of Intel Corporation came over their Internet last year? And did you know that one of the portals last year had five billion hits. And they can, today, predict, the advertising message you would like to give. They can give you an estimate of the number of hits you are going to get and the number of sales that you will make with a reasonably good and high statistical accuracy.

Finally I wanted you to see a videotape – time is short so I'll have to tell you about it – the videotape is of a young person playing a sophisticated game on the Internet. This person is simultaneously using another computer connected to the Internet to collect hints on how to win the game he is playing on the other one. It's a videotape of a five year old. What does that portend for the capacity of the next generation?

So those are my thoughts for you. I think that it is a very exciting time, a challenging time and one that I truly look forward to.

Now, we are going to seek some views of our distinguished panel. Do our industries truly need more standards, and if so, what are the kinds of standards that are missing? Is there anyone on the panel that would like to tackle what should the industry broadly defined do next?

Craig Schnuck: I can answer that. It really varies by industry, and the challenge we have had for a number of years with the code council is that we are servicing so many different industries, and the needs are different in different industries because of where they are in terms of adoption of the code as well as changes that are occurring in each of those industries. So that's not a very simple question to answer. We've been trying to take communications standards that were originally developed for the supermarket industry or for the general merchandise retail industry and transition them over to industrial and other commercial activities. Many of those have worked, others require further modification to make them work for the specific needs of that industry. So really it's a broad-based question, there are lots of different additional communications standards we need to develop to properly serve all industries we are presently working with and those that we'd like to begin to serve in the future. So there's a long laundry list of things we need to address.

Larry Russell: I think Tom Wilson had it right in one of the comments he made. Standards or the guidance of standards is the work of leaders, of C.E.O.'s and when left only to the technical part of the organization, it would seem to me that things don't get done as quickly, or as focused, as when the leadership takes hold and gives direction. Maybe that's another dimension to the challenge of defining. Ted.

Ted Rybeck: Yes, to build on what you just said, Dave for instance had gotten the UCC involved with RosettaNet (a consortium of electronic equipment manufacturers and distributors) which is doing some provocative things in the high tech supply chain. What we're finding is, especially for the dot com e-tailers, because that's a clicks and mortar orientation as Dave and I were saying, a lot of them are building out their back end (distribution processes) now. The U.P.C. plays a very different role for them. All of a sudden a lot of the logistics issues that the UCC has been working on, come up. Then, if you look at the exchanges that are being developed on the B to B, business to business relationships, all of a sudden you are at click and mortar again, because the traditional distribution and logistics frameworks are changing. So the biggest area we've seen a need for is the bridge between the conventional retail and distribution channels. This is clicks and mortar integration. It's not as though the Amazons and Dells aren't actually having to worry about what's behind the curtain – they're addressing that now, but they need the UCC's help.

Alan L. Haberman: We've spent twenty-five years just working out the implications of that little footprint of the U.P.C. symbol itself, our core standard and we still haven't finished, not by a long shot. We extrapolate from it and make standards of the best business practices of the industries we serve. But now we're in a new paradigm. They've changed it on us; they've pulled the rug out from underneath us. We're not going to have time to finish the old course, before we wrench it around to chase a new horizon.

Okay, that work is dependent upon how well an industry – the members of an industry – talk to us and, through us, to each other. Always it will be dependent on whether they recognize their problems, whether there is a structure through which they give us, gather for themselves the necessary information, and ask the necessary questions. It is a two-sided job, we lead, they lead, we do it together. We are experts at nurturing this cooperative system – there are few others like us in this world.

You asked how do we interface with the dot-coms at this point, and let them know what our capabilities are? We know how to organize an industry, are experts at seeing relationships. We can go back out and sell our capabilities. We have to find them and proselytize. That's one piece of it, but we've got the other thing to do as well – energize as best we can those industries that we serve today. That is our strength and it will appeal to the new dot-coms and bring them to us. We can energize industry councils, help them work out the answers from which we bring forth standards and interoperability. It's a two-sided thing, and yeah, we've got to discard a lot of things we're doing, but never the techniques we use to foster cooperation and sharing. We've got to get those councils going as never before. I think Ralph Dryer of P&G is working on one right now – one that is global in scope. Great! Let's get more forums going. With these organized groups we can examine what this e-business is all about.

I have one seemingly simple but most complex piece I think the UCC can do and may be the only one that can – and that is to sit down with its industries and decide on their product dictionary. Ease of transaction in the e world requires consistency: What category does an item belong to, what kinds of information about it must be available, how much space can it reasonably require to express the needed data? Unless we can work it with industry, there are dot-coms out there that will make it their preserve and chaos could be the result of their need for speed and ownership. I think that Tom Rittenhouse is looking at the area, that Paul Benchner is looking at, as he established the priorities for the UCC interface with the extranet.

Lawrence C. Russell: Louis H. Borders may be the newest and unlikeliest member of the Internet new economy. After all, the fifty-one-year-old entrepreneur is known as the man behind bookseller Border's group, the second largest bookstore chain in the U.S. What does he know about doing business in cyberspace? Turns out he's got an idea compelling enough to lure more than $120 million from hallmark investors such as CBS, Yahoo, Softbank, and venerable venture capital firms like Sequoia Capital and Benchmark Capital. Now he's banking on something, that he's going to be one of the biggest home delivery providers of perishable groceries and food in the United States. He's looking to take a piece of the $720 billion industry. Now a couple of interesting things. He plans to be able to fulfill and deliver in thirty minutes. It's right here in the article. He plans to offer – he plans to be able to pick a twenty-five-item order out of a total of 50,000 available products in less than hour. And he's backed by serious money. And he's not a bad retailer, although he probably doesn't know a lot about beans. But the money's there, and I've been talking to some of the people in the industry, and sure enough, home delivery looks like it's working – Peapod, Homegrocer.com – it looks like the economics are shifting. For years and years we talked about it. Anybody worried here?

Alan L. Haberman: I'd like to comment on this. Fifteen years ago I did a model of home order/delivery for Trintex, a joint venture of CBS, IBM and Sears, and I had to expose some of the people in this room to that model in trying to sell them what became and is now Prodigy. The economics have always been there. There's no question – it can be done cheaper. Does the customer want it? Are they willing to buy their groceries that way? Some of them are. But it is not just a grocery business anymore. It's more than a grocery business. It is how you can deliver all kinds of goods and services to the home and handle the transportation part. What fascinates me now is how most of our retailers are sitting and allowing a group of people out there who've got nothing but an idea and piles of money from J.P. Morgan and the market to go in and try to build the reputation for expertise and quality and service that is the retailer's birthright and is required for the transition from store purchase to home delivery. That bothers me. It bothers me that the founder of Border's can raise the kind of money for food that boggles the imagination and no one in the supermarket industry and/or the department store industry until very recently was willing to risk their own capital and capitalize on their capabilities, or have not yet, found the financial formula that would have Wall Street share in the risk. What a shame.

Lawrence C. Russell: I'll bet there's a lot of customers in the grocery stores, in the companies you represent, who you're not so hot about serving. How about in the banking industry for example? Fully 20 percent of the customers lose an amount of money equal to what an average retail bank makes today. The top 20 percent earn from 120 percent to 140 percent of what a bank makes. The worst 20 percent lose about what the company makes. And by the way, demographics, there is zero correlation with demographics. It's not the wealthy people that make the banks rich. There is no correlation, none. I've done it ten times over, and with all the big banks you can imagine. So do they want those loser customers? Let's get rid of them. Let's let somebody else do it, a branchless bank.

Dave Carlson: Let me take a different tack though. When today's five year old is twenty-three, he or she is not going to walk down a supermarket gathering cans of Campbell's soup. He's not going to do it. There is no value if they can click, click, click and have it delivered. Again, brick and mortar versus click and order. They are immensely comfortable, in fact far more comfortable in that environment or will be, than taking a grocery trolley down through the lanes of a supermarket. And by the way, far more efficient if you already set up your order, scan items as they go into the discard, and your preset order is already there. The paradigm shift is absolutely happening. One of the discouraging things, both today and the e-com conference in Phoenix five months ago, is that the food industry may not "get it." There is a massive paradigm shift occurring, and if you're shopping on the Internet, you don't need the little code. And this industry, it seems to me, has to come to grips with that. Thank God we've got somebody like Haberman who just sticks it to us every time he gets a chance.

Alan L. Haberman: There is no need to make the decision; there is no need to agree that you're right. It's a big world; there's a big market out there. There are people that will buy this way. You don't have to kiss the stores goodbye. Things are done in incremental bits. Just don't let somebody else take it away from you.

Dave Carlson: Look at the ukrop.com site, and you'll begin to see something that's going on in kind of hybrid customer service through brick and mortar and customer service through click and order.

Craig Schnuck: We're doing very much the same thing Dave. We're doing home delivery now via Internet ordering.

Dave Carlson: Terrific.

Craig Schnuck: We're doing it in every market area in which we do business, and it's being serviced from the stores.

Dave Carlson: That's why you're on the panel right?

Craig Schnuck: Maybe. The technologies that Webvan developed, the warehouse will work. The ability to select orders, individual units, from over 50,000 items can be done. Their ability to deliver on a cost-effective basis within thirty minutes anywhere, that's one part I have a real question about. And that part really remains to be seen if they can effectively do that in a half hour time frame.

Alan L. Haberman: It's not necessary.

Craig Schnuck: The other part of it is, even if they are tremendously successful, and reach the kind of market penetration that they're shooting for, they'll still represent less than two percent of the industry. So I'm not saying we should therefore ignore them; we still need to watch them. That's one of the reasons that we're active in home delivery through the Internet, because we want to be there. If that's what the customer wants to be, we want to be there and provide that service and provide those products to them. But it's not something that we've got to run and hide and say the whole industry is going to come down in a shambles because Webvan is going to come in and march all over everyone.

Lawrence C. Russell: Tom, do we have time for another question, or do you want to cut it here? Five minutes.

Ted Rybeck: Just to build on what Craig said. If we distinguish between what's happening in the industry, which we all have different feelings about, and what the UCC needs to do, I think it would be useful. Let's think about that. I wish there were a way that we could say, let's put aside our competitive disadvantages. At the UCC we have a strong tradition of bricks and mortar retailers and consumer goods suppliers to those retailers. That's going to prejudice the view of the UCC.

That can also be a strength, that tradition, but it's got to be carefully managed to keep it as a strength. Right now I think it's probably a disadvantage. As a person who has tremendous respect for the UCC and wants to see its leadership continue, I believe there needs to be an embracing of those new models, even beyond what we think their success might or might not be. Go beyond them in terms of embracing them. For example, what Craig did, and many others in this room did, to bring the Europeans and the North Americans together in worldwide standards. That's exactly what the Internet models for B to B and B to C need. And the UCC can provide that. The Internet companies and the venture capitalists behind them don't even know the UCC was up to that work.

Alan L. Haberman: And that's what that new generation up there is going to do under Tom Rittenhouse, UCC's president. They'd better shake what we've done loose, and I'm going to be there to make sure they do.

Lawrence C. Russell: Ken Omhie wrote the book entitled, *A Borderless World* and right now, Germany is at war with AOL because Amazon is delivering books into Germany that the German's don't want delivered there. By the way, how does a sovereign nation control goods and services when purchased through the Internet? Drugs, even good drugs, how does anybody hope to control the flow of goods in a borderless world. I don't know.

Last question, or do we have two minutes, here we go. This is an easy one. Is there room for a more innovative, e.g., debit card that functions as a preferred customer card or possibly a manufacturers preferred card that can be loaded with price promotions and facilitate saleable and available POS data. Maybe category cards, maybe multi-distributor cards. It could store promotions, it could collect information, and it could be inserted into a phone and could transmit the information back so you could in effect have a walking panelist. Is there room for something of that nature to truly take advantage of the technology that's here now and the fracturing natures of the consumers that we all depend on for our livelihoods?

Alan L. Haberman: In Europe, they're going crazy with smart cards and ID cards. If you want to, you can fill your wallet and five other wallets with smart cards, all of which have money and or personal ID involved. Someday, they'll come together – all data on one or a few cards. The question in my mind is – does the customer really want all the stuff which is possible? I don't know, but the capability is there – and many standards are already set. ISO/IEC JTC1/SC17, the large international standards organization committee that makes standards for credit cards and the like has also created international standards for smart cards.. You can do it, even if micro payments are involved – the penny and quarter are included in the micro payment standards just announced in the U.S. All of the mechanism is going into place for what you are calling for, yet I think the customer is going to reject it in some part at least. Privacy is the price to be paid. There are great risks to participation, I'm afraid as I take my chances. But I want to be there, need to be there, for my customers. I want to help the consumer find the necessary protections as they enjoy the rational benefits of technology.

Lawrence C. Russell: Well, I guess that's it, I want to thank you for letting me be with you, it's been a great pleasure and an honor to have been associated with this project. It's been a great pleasure to be here with all of you today to celebrate it.

CRACKING THE CODE

MARVIN L. MANN

WITHOUT THE ADVANCEMENTS INVOLVING LASERS AND MICROCHIPS, THE DEVELOPMENT OF THE UNIVERSAL PRODUCT CODE AND THE DREAM OF AN AUTOMATED CHECKOUT WOULD NOT HAVE BEEN POSSIBLE. THERE WAS A CODE, THERE WAS A SYMBOL, BUT THERE WAS NO EQUIPMENT OR SYSTEMS TO READ THE U.P.C. AFTER TAKING RISKS TO DEVELOP SCANNER EQUIPMENT AROUND THE GUIDELINES SET FORTH BY THE AD HOC COMMITTEE, IBM SHARED ITS TECHNOLOGY IN AN ATTEMPT TO BETTER THE GROCERY INDUSTRY.

MARVIN MANN SHARES HIS UNIQUE VANTAGE POINT AS A KEY CONTRIBUTOR TO THE DEVELOPMENT OF THE FIRST SCANNER AT IBM. MR. MANN SPEAKS ABOUT THE WORK OF THE AD HOC COMMITTEE AND HOW ITS FINDINGS WERE INTEGRAL IN DEVELOPING APPLIANCES FOR THE AUTOMATED CHECKOUT.

When someone refers to "cracking the code," you probably think of spy movies or deciphering enemy messages during war-times. Well, the U.P.C. project wasn't quite at that level, but there were a number of codes to crack and problems to solve along the way.

What was the world like before U.P.C.? The world and the neighborhood grocery store, and even the supermarket were much different places in 1973. The stores were smaller. There were far fewer items available than carried by the typical store today and the business was more labor intensive and less sophisticated. Labor costs were eating into the already-thin profit margins. Accurate inventory tracking was something on the wish list. Someone had to price every single item before it could be put on the shelf and the out-of-stock condition was horrendous in many stores. For the customer, the shopping trip was often a slow and tedious process. At the checkout, every item had to be picked up, the price had to be viewed and keyed into the register. While some checkers were amazingly fast, they were the exception, not the rule.

Let me side step a moment and tell a little side story about fast checkers. We were doing a checkout study with Safeway at the time and were ready to do some analysis of key entry, the standard register approach, versus scanning systems. We asked if they would let us have some checkers we could use as a benchmark to measure against. As a reward and a prize for the checkers in the Safeway organization, they picked the three best they had and sent them to Raleigh, North Carolina to be the benchmark. Well, the scanner could hardly beat them they were so good . . . but they were never the ones checking out my groceries!

Now, back to 1973. The register tape was only slightly better than a useless piece of paper. Dozens of items were identified as "grocery" or "produce" at best, along with their prices. Often the tapes weren't very readable. Worse yet, too often the item wasn't rung up and never put into the bag. There had to be a better way and there was, though I don't believe that any of us who were involved could imagine how ubiquitous the Universal Product Code symbol and bar coding would become. The U.P. C. spread from soft drinks and cereal in the grocery stores to mass merchandisers and finally the big department stores, and from there on to almost everything imaginable on the retail shelf.

It is about as difficult for me to imagine a world without the U.P.C. as one without personal computers. Each was developed at about the same time. And the advent of the personal computer and its growth has made the use of U.P.C. scanning viable in even the smallest stores – and a lot less expensive in all stores. The development and standardization of the U.P.C. happened with amazing speed and there was tremendous development in technology and systems that made its acceptance possible.

At the beginning of the 1970s the supermarket industry was facing some serious challenges. Labor costs were high and inventory control was difficult. With minimal profit margins, even a moderate improvement in labor costs, stocking, and inaccuracies at the checkout line could have a significant impact on a store's profit – or, as ultimately happened, on prices and on customer service and satisfaction. Supermarket technology at the time was an oxymoron.

There had been isolated attempts to automate the checkout process, but tests had found no cost-efficient or practical solution. Advances were fairly limited. The electronic cash register, like the electronic typewriter, was still basically a mechanical or electromechanical instrument with limited capabilities. While new technology was adopted early in food manufacturing and grocery warehouse and distribution operations, it had simply bypassed the grocery store. It was up to the leaders of the industry who had a vision of the possible to change the status quo.

The success of the U.P.C. project started with the creation of the Ad Hoc Committee in 1971. Not only were there representatives from some of the most influential organizations in the industry, but they were people who would make decisions. And, they were people who could influence others in their industry. As you know, this wasn't a large group and that was fortunate, because this small organization contributed to fast action. This job was done in an amazingly small amount of time. To the members' credit, there was little political maneuvering and pushing of individual agendas. They were working together as a team for the industry.

It was a huge undertaking to get the food manufacturers, the retailers, and the technology companies to work together. They needed not only to design, develop, test and select a common code that could be printed at little cost and scanned accurately at high speeds without the requirement for orientation, but at the same time, to visualize the system software and hardware required to motivate these groups to make the necessary investments. It was a big job. They had to demonstrate to everyone involved the financial results that would make the investments worthwhile.

There were myriad issues that developed along the way in addressing those challenges. For example, eliminating price marking. In California, the legislature got involved, and a few other states outlawed it. And an issue that was raised near the end of the project was laser beam exposure and eye safety. There was concern, especially on the part of the unions, about checkers who would be would be exposed to the lasers for hours at a time, and about the exposure to the shoppers and their children. At the time no one had studied the long-term effects of low-level lasers on the eyes. An expert on lasers at Stanford Research Institute (SRI) was commissioned to do a study and fortunately found no problems.

As the project began moving forward, the committee called on some of the leading technology companies of the day – OBM, NCR, RCA, Singer, Pitney Bowes, Unisys, and others. The committee had identified what was needed, and asked each of the technology companies to provide a solution. RCA and Kroger were already experimenting with a bull's-eye symbol. There had been some product coding on packaging and packing cartons since the 1950s, but this was the first broad-scale attempt to develop new technology for this purpose and try to standardize it. A broad view was vital to success. It wasn't just about scanning groceries at the checkout line. A standardized product identification system was key to unlocking a wide range of applications and technology, which would impact the entire logistical chain, providing benefits across most operations from the manufacturer to the retailer to the consumer. An understanding of new applications that were envisioned and financial analysis and quantification of the key benefits was required. The financial analysis was key to motivating the industries to make the required investments.

Although today we're marking the twenty-fifth anniversary of the first commercial installation of U.P.C. scanning equipment, the story actually started in 1947. As you know, that was when Joe Woodland, sitting on a beach in Miami, pondering how to eliminate checkout errors, put his fingers in the sand and drew a set of lines – and the lightbulb came on. Joe drew a set of circular lines in the sand and the bull's-eye symbol idea was born. Joe tells me that what caused him to do that was that the people from Food Fair had visited him at Drexel University and talked about the problem they were having with shrinkage. They were losing about one percent of revenues at the checkout counter. They had the idea that if they had an automated checkout, they might be able to help solve this problem. So Joe was thinking about this challenge on the beach.

By 1952, Joe and Bob Silver, an electrical engineer and Joe's former colleague on the faculty at Drexel, had a patent for the symbol and a scanner that would read it. Joe subsequently received special recognition from the President George H.W. Bush, for his inventiveness – The 1992 National Medal of Technology. Joe and Bob were about twenty years ahead of their time. And think about this – the laser and the computer chip, essential parts of today's U.P.C. system, hadn't even been invented. Soon afterward, Joe joined IBM and during the mid-1950s led a research and development effort in Westchester Country, New York, and further developed the bull's-eye system. Unfortunately, the cost-benefit analysis wasn't favorable, but Joe learned a lot about the potential benefit of scanning systems. And this knowledge became valuable during our work in the early 1970s. Eventually, as you know, Bob and Joe sold their patent to Philco, who then sold it to RCA.

How do we go from the bull's-eye to the vertical bars that we know about today? Actually there were a number of symbols that could have been chosen. The Ad Hoc Committee received fourteen different proposals that included bars, circles, and parts of circles. The first thing to settle, however, was the underlying numerical system to support the symbol. Once the basis of the numerical system was in place, the design or appearance of the symbol, the most recognizable part to the consumer had to be determined. RCA had taken Joe Woodland's bull's-eye design and was working with Kroger at stores in the Cincinnati area. The system was proving the underlying concept of a productivity gain at the checkout.

IBM, meanwhile, was studying another run at the electronic cash register business. This is how I happened to become involved in the U.P.C. around 1970. IBM marketing executives within the distribution industry division had asked me to become project manager for – because they couldn't think of a better title – something they called "consumer transaction systems." This name was supposed to obscure the early market studies and technology efforts to develop retail point of sale systems. IBM had made a sizeable investment in an electromechanical cash register in the mid-1960s, but it died of its own weight, literally; it weighted sixty pounds.

Technology had advanced and IBM had begun to envision a big opportunity in retail store systems development. The marketing side of my team needed to help determine whether IBM should continue to invest in this opportunity and develop a plan for success. Under the leadership of Bill Carey, they began the intensive market requirements and financial analysis work that was to provide the important input to our decisions and to the U.P.C. work. The research and development team, under Paul McEnroe, was already developing the base technologies, such as the universal controller, or computer; the local area network for the store – probably the first local area network; the first application-oriented custom chip that was ever developed; the first IBM intelligent terminal (the cash register); printers, file technology and on and on. But the focus at that point was primarily on a key entry approach using a numerical item code with price look-up. For general merchandise stores, a magnetic stripe ticket containing the SKU (Stock Keeping Unit) number and price was to be the standard. These were to be proprietary systems. Feasibility was being studied with Safeway and Sears, and a little later with Dillard's, Supermarkets General, Wegman's, J. C. Penney, and others.

When the U.P.C. symbol selection committee came for a visit, it quickly became clear to me and the team that IBM needed to become involved if we wanted to help insure that the coding system selected was both technically and economically feasible. Work had already begun at IBM in California on bar code technology in the 1960s and work on a bar code began in Raleigh, North Carolina, which was the center of this work, in about 1970. But it was clear, based on conversations with the symbol selection subcommittee that more resources needed to be devoted and work accelerated on scanning and bar codes. The product planners at the time weren't too anxious to allocate the resources, preferring instead to continue on the key entry and magnetic stripe path. They had little confidence in the industry's ability to make this standardization effort successful. With the help of Bob Evans, who was division president at the time and Paul McEnroe, who was the consumer transaction systems development manager, the direction was changed on the system for supermarkets.

I'll pause to tell you a little bit of an inside story here. About 1969, Paul, who had done scanner development work earlier in his career, was ready to start a small unfunded effort in the laboratory to experiment with scanner development. Soon after, Bob Evans, the president of the development division, visited the lab. Paul took him back to show him a cardboard model of his scanner idea and told him about the code, which would be placed on the package. The code would be scanned, the price looked up in the computer file, and the item would be registered and priced for the customer. Bob Evans, who ultimately became vice president of research and development for IBM, was a very bright and technically competent executive. He looked at the model and listened to Paul's story and said, "Paul, this will never work." Now Paul's a pretty persuasive guy, and he had Bob's respect. After some debate and discussion Bob agreed with Paul that he would fund the effort for a year. A year later he would come back to North Carolina to review the progress. He said if it wasn't working to prove the concept the project would be terminated and Paul's desk would be moved out into the street. Talk about motivation – that was motivation. Well, a year later, Bob did go back to Raleigh and Paul handed him a package of cigarettes and Bob threw it across the scanner – spinning it on purpose – and it went "bing" and printed out the brand of cigarettes and the cost. Bob looked underneath the platform that this equipment was sitting on to see who might be under there operating this machine. That's literally true. From that point on, the program was on its way.

With RCA apparently having a head start, IBM's engineering team had to move rapidly to develop equipment to support the symbol. George Laurer, an outstanding IBM engineer and now retired senior engineer scientist, had some unusual and untried ideas. He believed the bar code had significant advantages over the bull's-eye, especially in printing. He began to build on earlier bar code design ideas and adapt them to meet the industry's needs. Joe Woodland was in frequent contact with the symbol selection committee, gathering input about the requirements, and George was working on the details of developing that code. Now this bar code had some advantages. It could be made smaller than the bull's-eye, an important point with package designers. Like the circular bull's-eye, a scanner could read it from various angles, increasing productivity. And it was adaptable to widely varying printing requirements, which was the make-or-break issue for any of the proposed symbols and probably the greatest advantage that the IBM symbol had.

Printing was the critical issue. The U.P.C. had to appear on boxes produced by numerous printers, some better than others. It would be on bags. It would be on packages for meat and produce. It would be on cans. It would get wrinkled and stretched. It would be printed on high-speed web presses, high-quality sheetfed presses, some slow and low-quality presses, and even on in-store printers. Distortions in the symbol would mean failures to scan, which would impact productivity and could create errors in the scan. Because nearly every grocery package included the words "net weight," hundreds of packages were sent to IBM's laboratory in Rochester, Minnesota. There, variances in printing of the letter "t" in "net weight" were measured and used to establish standards for the printing of the symbol.

A design called the Delta Distance System was adopted to take into account distortions in the printing of the symbol. The Delta Distance System would work regardless of the symbol's size, and dimensional tolerances were essentially eliminated, a very important characteristic of the symbol. Rather than having scanners measure the width of the bars, which could be individually distorted, they instead measured the distance between the leading and trailing edges of each bar from that of the following bar. The nature of the printing process, with paper always being fed at an orientation guaranteeing the edges of the symbol wouldn't blur, meant that they would always be consistent, assuring an accurate scan. The ability to read the proposed symbol using various printing processes, substrates, coatings, and variations in printing accuracy was being measured using IBM's Pictorial Information Dissector and Analyzer (PIDAS) measurement system in Minnesota.

George Laurer's design included a number of features that made it a superior design. For example, he had the same number of bars in each digit, in each character. He had the same number of bars in each symbol.

Now think about this. That dumb scanner had to look at the package – everything on the package – and figure out where the bar code was and which kind of bar code was on the package. It could find that bar code because it knew how many lines were in it and how many bars were in it. Another thing that George designed into the symbol was to allow for single-error correction. That is, if the scanner didn't read properly, it could correct one digit read in incorrectly. And it could detect reading two digits in error and stop or go back and scan it again. Incidentally, George came up with the revolving mirror concept for the scanners, which was a real breakthrough in terms of getting a high-speed scanner at low cost. Technology evaluations were also conducted by MIT in an effort to consider future technological implications of the alternative code submissions.

By this time, we were frequently meeting with the symbol selection subcommittee to demonstrate to them that the IBM Delta Distance System was the right solution for accurate and inexpensive printing and scanning. The symbol selection workgroup was made up of people committed to finding the best solution and they did an outstanding job. Several of the members of the group are here tonight and they were recognized earlier today by Larry Russell. Al Haberman, who chaired the subcommittee, was always driving us to the wall, to work and to get the right answers. He was challenging us continuously. Eric Waldbaum, Barry Franz, and Fritz Biermeier understood what they were seeing, hearing, and learning, and were able to make objective comparisons of all of the alternative candidates and systems. Larry Russell was not a member of this subcommittee, but he was supporting the subcommittee and, as you know, he was a senior associate at McKinsey and Company at the time. He's a visionary who has the ability to dig into and understand the minute details that were necessary to understand for this task and many others that he's tackled through the years. In my opinion, he is due a significant amount of the credit for this achievement. He really was a very key player.

While we were working with the committee and retailers supporting their financial feasibility analysis, Bill Carey, Joe Woodland, and their associates were working in parallel with other retailers to be sure that the business case was solid and the retailers would buy in. I might add that we were making enormous investments by this point in time and that we had to be sure that the business case was solid and that people were going to buy and get their money out of these systems.

A team of software development people was working in Chicago, under Paul Day's leadership, developing software to drive the "soft benefits" – utilizing the item movement data to automate ordering, lower inventory investments, reduce stockouts, cut shrink, and improve labor scheduling. The development team in Raleigh was working diligently to define the myriad details to program all of the code with every conceivable option to manage every function in the wide variety of retail stores, including a back-up system to prevent failures. At that time the computer had about 32,000 bytes of memory. That was an improvement because earlier it was only 16,000 bytes. Contrast that with the PC that you buy for a few hundred dollars today that has 32, 64 or 128 megabytes of memory. Because memory was very expensive then, we were forced to put all of that application code to run the store operations in the firmware of the computer. And if there were any other alternative, one wouldn't choose to do that.

We developed duplex systems, but the price for a duplex system made it too expensive for all but the largest stores. So a system was developed whereby a store with only a single controller could, over a telephone line, dial into a sister store and pick up that controller and back itself up. This provided a solution for somewhat smaller stores. But in spite of all that work when we began to install systems we had some failures. And the backup system, even the fully duplexed in-store system, failed at times.

Bob Martin of Wal-Mart was often on the telephone to me, and at times I wished I could turn the volume down. He was telling me in every way imaginable that it was unacceptable to have a Wal-Mart store out of business. I want to tell him now that I knew that, I just didn't know how to fix it. I couldn't argue the point at all. Those were some dark days. We invited IBM's engineers, who were working on the NASA project, which just couldn't fail for any reason, to come and help us design solutions and develop the answer to this problem, which ultimately we put in place.

Just before the U.P.C. council made its selection IBM was asked if it would give its code to the industry, if it were chosen, with no strings attached. After all of the tremendous efforts of people and the major investments they had made, IBM just hadn't given much thought to giving it away. But after some discussions, logic prevailed. The code was given away and the IBM proposal was selected.

Soon after we began shipping pilot systems to the stores, it became clear that things weren't working out quite as we planned. There were all kinds of new and unforeseen difficulties. I would like to give you some insight, retrospectively, into some of the things that happened that eventually helped make these systems work. I was managing the sales, marketing and application software development efforts and was responsible for customer satisfaction. I want to tell you, there wasn't a lot of the latter in those early days. I was constantly meeting with the product management and development team to get them to add resources, which they didn't have authorization to do, and solve these deficiencies. I was coming on so strong that one day in the heat of the battle one of the higher-level development executives, Paul's boss's boss, told me in a very loud voice that he was going to do everything in his power to get me fired, to get me off his back. Well, soon after that, I got a call from Bob Evans. He asked if I could come and visit with him in his office. We were in different divisions. This didn't sound good. But to my great surprise he said he wanted me to take over responsibility for total product management and do whatever it took to make this business successful – reporting to the man who was anxious to get me fired. Refer to Professor Dunlop's chart today depicting the slow buildup of scanning systems in use in supermarkets during the period from 1974 through 1977. We had invested a lot of IBM's money in these systems. I want to tell you that there were several occasions when I presented the financial results in a program review with the top executives at IBM, when the odds were in favor of early termination of my career.

Well, I was able to persuade them each time that gold was at the end of the rainbow, and it was. Well maybe not gold, but silver anyway. Several months ago on the twenty-fifth anniversary of the announcement of the first IBM retail store system, which was 1973, I was invited to attend a meeting in Raleigh of people who had worked in this group through the years. People came from everywhere. Numerous people who were part of the effort twenty-five years ago are still involved. Others have retired and some have moved on to new jobs in other organizations, many of them in organizations in or in support of the retail industry. It was great to reminisce and talk about what had happened. They asked me to make some remarks at the meeting and I was pleased to say that IBM, several years earlier, had gained the number one share position in retail systems in the world. They'd come a long way. And as I reflected on this event, it was clear to me that the reason for that success and the ultimate success of IBM's store system was due to the excellent management and outstanding people. But further, it was due to an organization structure which was somewhat unique in IBM. An organization structure that provided a tremendous focus on this market, on this set of systems, with continuity. By that I mean with people who stayed with it over years and years, and learned and learned.

The business structure of the IBM retail systems organization was almost unique in IBM. It conceptually integrated software and hardware development, manufacturing, marketing, sales, service and the support team. This structure resulted in a tight communications loop, in a constant learning process with close communication between the sales and marketing people and highly responsive development, manufacturing and support people to meet the customers' evolving needs. Each new generation of technology was used to implement what was learned from working with customers, constantly increasing the financial benefits by adding new functions and applications, improving reliability, increasing capacity and performance, and reducing costs and prices.

I would like to express my appreciation to some of these outstanding people who represent a much larger group of IBM people. Paul McEnroe, Joe Woodland, George Laurer, Bill Carey, and a person whose name has not been mentioned, who was a key member supporting IBM efforts in support of the VICS committee, which came a bit later, Bill Jones. There was a commitment among this team to do whatever it took to meet customers' needs.

Now as an aside, to talk about lessons learned, this experience with a highly focused market-oriented, integrated organization was used to implement a very similar approach at Lexmark International when this company was spun out of IBM in 1991. And some people would say a printer company? Market focused? Well, let me tell you that in eight years we took this company from slightly more than zero share in the printer business to the number two position in the world market in corporate laser printers, and a major player in the consumer printer market.

We hold the largest share in the world in key market segments, such as the retail industry's use of Lexmark laser printers in retail stores and in other key market segments. A key printing application in retail stores using Lexmark printers is printing U.P.C. labels. We know how to do that pretty well by now; we've had a lot of experience. As a result, to a meaningful degree of what we learned in these earlier retail efforts, Lexmark's market value has grown from about $450 million eight years ago to more than $11 billion today. And the price of Lexmark stock has increased 2,500 percent since we started in 1991, and more than 800 percent since we took the company public in November of 1995, a little less than four years ago.

The U.P.C. effort that began almost thirty years ago has been more successful, certainly, than could have been imagined. The dramatic advancements in technology and the systems developed have brought enormous benefits to the industry as a result of the successful and yes, ubiquitous, implementation of the code. But more is possible, I believe. While almost all companies are enjoying significant benefits, not nearly as many companies, particularly in the food industry, I'm told, are taking real advantage of the availability of so much useful data that is generated by scanning the code. More can be done.

When you think about it, there was only a small number of people, outstanding people, but a small number, who did the work that made it possible to have the U.P.C. You know, it makes me wonder, and some have alluded to this today, why this effort wouldn't be an excellent road map for other standards efforts – perhaps not all, but some. For example, it seems to me that the healthcare industry cries out for just such an initiative.

In my view the characteristics and the character of the Ad Hoc Committee and the U.P.C. development team are reflective of a vital free enterprise system that never allowed ego to negatively influence the greater good that can come from truly great ideas. Will there be hurdles? Sure. Will there always be agendas that stand at odds? Of course. But in the case of the U.P.C. effort, through these complex and at times vexing challenges, there remained a sense of purpose, a mission that prompted us to forge ahead to solve this set of challenges – to crack the code.

As you might have guessed by now, I'm not a person who shies away from a challenge. But I'd be lying to you if I were to say I didn't have moments of doubt along the way. But when I look back on this effort and see the power that one idea and hard work and some compromise and tenacity can deliver I feel very fortunate to count myself among those who played even a small part in solving this problem.

I would like to congratulate the members of the U.P.C. Council, and the symbol selection sub-committee, my IBM colleagues, and all of the industry people involved who contributed through the years to achieving such tremendous success and benefits. Who would have thought that our lives would be defined, in part, by small lines that only a few human eyes can read?

We really did crack the code, didn't we?

After the Bar Code,
What Next?

Steven N. David,
Global Customer Business Development
Officer,
The Procter & Gamble Company

and

Thomas S. Rittenhouse
President and Chief Executive Officer,
Uniform Code Council, inc.

Steve David

It gives me enormous pleasure to be here at the Smithsonian to celebrate the twenty-fifth anniversary of U.P.C. – an innovation that had an enormous impact on our industry.

In a few moments I would like to join with Tom Rittenhouse to make a special announcement concerning the future. But first, I want to talk about the vision and spirit that gave birth to the success we are celebrating here today. At Procter & Gamble, we pride ourselves on leadership, creativity and innovation. The bar code is a terrific example of all three.

The U.P.C was first conceived at the end of the 1960s. Neil Armstrong had just walked on the moon. Few people had heard of silicon chips. Computers were rare. Lasers barely existed outside laboratories. And yet, a small group of people had the courage and imagination to conceive of a future where every checkout counter in every store would contain a laser, would be attached to a computer, and would automatically read bar codes.

Most people must have thought these pioneers were crazy. Many laughed at them and their vision. But despite this, the bar code's founding fathers were able to create within their own companies, and then their industries, a broad consensus that their studied solution could and should be implemented. With that consensus the dream became real, creating the success we are celebrating here today: a revolution so complete, so global, that we now find it hard to imagine the world any other way.

Which brings me to the future. When the bar code was being developed, a committee of scientists at the Massachusetts Institute of Technology – its chairman, Professor Murray Eden, is also with us today – was asked to assess how long it would be before the technology would need an upgrade. The answer? 25 years!

So today as we recognize the twenty-fifth anniversary of that technology, it is fitting to ask this question: After the bar code, what next?

Before I go any further, let me stress that I am not suggesting the end of the bar code. Bar codes are so successful and so deeply embedded in our systems that they will be with us for years to come. But, just as the pioneers of twenty-five years ago dared to imagine a radically new and better way of doing business, so should we.

For example, one answer to the question "what comes next?" might be a microchip embedded into every product. I know it sounds crazy today to imagine a world where every box of Tide, every package of Pampers, and every other product in the world has a microchip built into it, but it probably doesn't sound any more crazy than bar codes did back in 1970.

Now, I don't know if microchips are the future. This is just one exciting possibility. But I am sure of this: The time to start finding out what should come next is now, today. And we also need to find out how we can get to the future in a seamless, economical, consensus-building way.

I am also sure that we must take care to remember the crucial lessons of the bar code: Nothing drives information technology better, faster and further than standards; and the best standards are led and developed by end users. Industry should lead technology – it should not fall unprepared into the future. Using the U.P.C. process as our model for involvement and consensus we can discover the new technologies and build the new global standards that will energize us and the world in the coming century.

With these points in mind, I am pleased to be able to announce to you today the beginning of a new journey: The journey to discover what will follow the bar code.

On behalf of the Uniform Code Council, the Massachusetts Institute of Technology, and the Procter & Gamble Company, I am delighted to announce the creation of a new Worldwide Research Center that will develop our existing technologies further, and will examine and develop the new technologies upon which we will build the standards of the future.

The dollars P&G and the UCC today contribute to the new MIT Automatic Identification and Data Capture (AIDC) Center are the first of many that must and I am sure will follow from companies across the distribution industries. These dollars will create the technical and scientific arm for users around the world who strive together to reduce costs, increase efficiency, and drive innovation in industry for the benefit of consumers, shoppers, employees, and shareholders alike – continuing the work that began twenty-five years ago, when that first bar code was scanned in a Marsh Supermarket in Ohio.

Tom Rittenhouse

For over two years, UCC as been seeking the proper venue for a world class AIDC research center. In recent months we found that the Electronic Article Surveillances (EAS) initiative taken by you, Kodak, and Johnson and Johnson brought you to the same academic institutions we were working with to develop proposals for the Center concept. Your people immediately embraced UCC's broader objectives. We shared data and found that we had gravitated to the same MIT group of researchers that we eventually chose to manage the Center. I am indeed very grateful to you and those in your company who were so instrumental in making the choice and for their vision and leadership in the areas of standards and technology that brings you to jointly parent the Center.

The UCC exists to serve its members. Using our expertise in standards management, our mission is to guide industries of users through the consensus building process needed to create, promote, and maintain standards and the best practices that grow from them. We exist to aid you in delivering real business value – standards and practices that live, breathe, and are vibrant.

The inexorable and seemingly ever accelerating march of information, communication, materials, and process technology challenges our industries in ways we ignore at our peril. We must understand them, sort them down to those that best meet our needs, develop new capabilities that grow from them, and fit them seamlessly into our business structures. Witness the explosion of e-commerce. The extra net capabilities that UCC and the food industry are now developing, our not-for-profit subsidiary, *UCCnet,* is a child of these developments we all recognize as essential to our future. We must track potential change through the connecting links between our industries and businesses and respond in constructive and profitable ways.

We have long studied and now are convinced that the new research center is essential because it expands and organizes our capabilities, supplies us with an expertise we cannot wait for, or even begin to afford to build from scratch. It is the best possible vehicle for this work.

The Center will perform four primary functions:

- Develop the next generation of techniques and languages for automatic product identification and information management from which standards will be generated.
- Perform fundamental research in the applications of these systems in support of industry initiatives.
- Develop prototype application test-beds demonstrating advanced automatic identification technologies for specific industries.
- Continuously assess emerging technologies and act as an information and evaluation resource.

Although headquarters will be at the Massachusetts Institute of Technology here in the United States, this will not be an exclusive activity. As the word Center implies, it is the intent that work will be conducted globally, shared out to and received from the world's finest universities and research institutes. It will be gathered, perhaps guided and certainly communicated, by our Center. It will offer a worldview as befits the new global economy.

There is one central ingredient to the mix. The researcher cannot do his work alone, nor should he try to. As Steve so wisely reminds us, learning from the development of the bar code, the Center will be supported and guided by end users, and it will work closely with information technology developers and vendors and AIDC suppliers. A board of overseers will be selected from industry and those who contribute and a structure of committees will be created that will feed industry needs and vision to that Board so that Center research will be pointed and evaluated. In turn the results will be widely distributed so that they may affect and guide industries's visions of the future. You will be especially pleased to know that EAN will be an important part of the Center's constituency. It will share equally with UCC a seat on the Center's governance committee, thus adding great assurance that we will achieve the global reach that is so essential in today's distribution systems.

Procter & Gamble has already stepped forward, not only to energize its own vision with money, but by example, to point the way. P&G will contribute, in addition, the first of what will be a rotating series of industry donated business managers to the Center.

The hope is that other businesses will take this opportunity – not just in the world of consumer goods, nor only in the US, but in all industries and from any nation – to support the new Center and to share the same spirit of imagination, innovation and cooperation that gave us the bar code twenty-five years ago.

Our goal is a fund of between five and six million dollars as the base support for the Center, which will also on its own raise additional funds through contract research.

With the inauguration of the MIT AIDC Research Center today, we are assembled not only to celebrate the achievements of the past twenty-five years, but also to enthusiastically mark the beginning of a new, shared future that will benefit our industries and society. God willing, and with the cooperation of the medical community – perhaps enlivened by the ability to set their own standards for efficiency – I will still be around twenty-five years from now. If so, I expect to join a group which will be brought together to celebrate the anniversary of this, our auspicious new beginning and its far reaching successes.

Appendix

17 Billion Reasons to Say Thanks

INTRODUCTION

> We showed that it could be done on a massive scale, that cooperation without antitrust implications was possible for the common good, and that business didn't need the government to shove it in the right direction.
>
> — Alan Haberman, Chairman,
> Symbol Standardization Subcommittee[1]

With a swipe of the hand on June 26, 1974 at a Marsh supermarket in Troy, Ohio, a pack of chewing gum became the first retail product sold using a scanner and the Universal Product Code (U.P.C.) symbol. The result of decades of work, investment, and unprecedented cooperation in the grocery industry, the U.P.C. symbol today is generating $17 billion through the grocery channel alone in annual savings for manufacturers, retailers, and consumers.[2] Today, celebrating its twenty-fifth anniversary, the U.P.C. symbol as we have known it may be closer to its end than its beginning. With its planned phase out by 2005,[3] there is even greater reason to remember what was accomplished and to study the lessons that this historic event, the adoption of the U.P.C. symbol, can teach.

---

[1]"Bar Codes are Sweeping the Nation," *Invention & Technology,* Volume 8, Number 3, by Tony Seiderman.
[2]Benefits realized have been estimated by taking the same methodology used by McKinsey & Co. in 1973 and applying the methodology to the grocery industry in 1997.
[3]The Uniform Code Council members have to adopt the 13-digit EAN as well as U.P.C. at the point of sale beginning January 1, 2005.

More than simply a case of dollars and cents, the success of the U.P.C. was rooted in the entire grocery industry's foresight to think strategically and to collaborate in order to take advantage of the capabilities of new and emerging technologies. The results were industry-wide productivity enhancements, with minimal efforts wasted on technological dead ends. Further, the operation of the grocery industry as we know it today would be inconceivable without the information derived from tracking U.P.C. coded merchandise. Consider that in 1974, the average store carried 9,000 SKUs. In 1997, the average grocery store carried 30,000 SKUs. Despite the larger assortments, store managers are now far more able to control price changes, promotions, and product assortments than they were in the past. Yet, in spite of the billions of dollars in savings generated for the food industry, the full potential of the U.P.C. Symbol has yet to be realized.

Grocery stores have used the U.P.C. effectively to improve internal operations ranging from pricing to checkout scanning to inventory and assortment management. While the grocery industry has, to a great degree, focused primarily on using the U.P.C. for internal productivity enhancements, the industry has failed to capture the full value possible from the sharing of information among companies. In an industry with a rich history of combative supply–chain relationships, sharing of data to optimize the performance of the total system has been much slower to gain acceptance. This is in sharp contrast to the discount and general merchandise channels where, for example, the automatic transmission of point-of-sale (POS) data has been instrumental in reducing inventory, shortening lead times, and increasing profitability.

It was the widespread support for scanning in the grocery industry that initially justified the investment in the technology. Over time, scanner performance continued to improve dramatically while the cost of scanners decreased. As a result, annual savings realized in the grocery industry from the U.P.C. have exceeded many times over the benefits originally estimated. The irony in celebrating the success of the U.P.C. is that the grocery industry has remained content with its initial productivity gains while other channels and industries have taken the next step of extracting more of the information value from the collected tracking data. One consequence has been an erosion in market share for grocery retailers as other retail channels including discount stores, warehouse clubs, and super centers have more fully exploited the value of information generated from U.P.C. transactions to become more efficient operators.

LEARNING FROM THE U.P.C. DECISION

"I think the industry has sold itself on a program that offers so little return that it simply won't be worth the trouble and expense"

— A Midwest Chain Executive[4]

When we look ahead and try to envision how the standards we are setting today will affect business in the coming years, perhaps we should first learn from similar decisions made in the past. Our tendency is to look back on past decisions with 20/20 hindsight and view with a sense of inevitability the establishment and acceptance of an industry standard. Instead of taking the past for granted, we should take a hard look at what really made the U.P.C. effort successful and try to apply these lessons to our current efforts to improve the industry.

The U.P.C. Symbol, the personal computer, and even the Internet are all things that are integral parts of business strategy in 1999. However, as recently as five years ago, the Internet was viewed solely as a tool for research scientists and educational institutions. Only in the past ten years have personal computers became ubiquitous in the workplace. And in 1970, the question was whether the development of a Universal Product Code would be worth the effort.

Even then the concept of automated checkstands had been around for almost forty years. Experiments with scanning had been first completed in the early 1950s. And in the late 1960s, led by companies like Kroger, the technology for automated checkstands was beginning to move rapidly towards commercial reality.

The real story of the U.P.C. lies not so much in the symbol that was selected or the fact that a 10-digit, all-numeric code was approved. Rather, the real lessons that the U.P.C. provides center around how the grocery industry collaborated to move from a concept and a few pilot tests to the installation of millions of dollars worth of scanning equipment and the symbol marking of virtually 99 percent of all packaged goods.

[4]"Scanning Hits a Snag," *Progressive Grocer,* December 1975, p. 47.

OVERVIEW OF THE ADOPTION PROCESS

In the 1960s, development of standardized product codes proceeded through several uncoordinated efforts. Various manufacturers, wholesalers, retailers, and industry organizations had made efforts towards establishing bar codes that could be used to track the flow of product in the supply chain. These efforts failed because the participants could not resolve conflicts that arose based on the size of the code, compatibility with existing product codes at various firms, and the costs of conversion. Retailers preferred a shorter code, as they might have to key in the information at checkout. Meanwhile, manufacturers preferred longer codes that could contain more detailed product information and provide a reserve for future growth.

In 1970, the success of the Kroger/RCA/IMS automated store test rekindled the industry's interest in the potential for automated checkstands. However, it was not possible at the time to create scanners that could read multiple bar code symbols. As such, conversion to a scanner-enabled electronic front end would not be feasible without a standardized symbol to represent the standardized product codes.

The ability to read a bar code and store its identity in a computer creates little or no economic value unless the code is standardized so that many companies can also read and store the same information. This way, a symbol can be printed once and then read by every retailer in the system using similar hardware and software.

On August 25, 1970, representatives of member organizations of the Distributor and Manufacturer Association formed The Grocery Industry Ad Hoc Committee. The newly formed Ad Hoc Committee was charged with the task of studying and reporting on the economic potential of a Universal Product Code along with the potential roadblocks implementation in the grocery industry would encounter. Organizations represented included:

- Cooperative Food Distributors of America (CFDA)
- Grocery Manufacturers of America (GMA)
- National American Wholesale Grocers' Association (NAWGA)
- National Association of Food Chains (NAFC)

- National Association of Retail Grocers (NARGUS)
- Supermarket Institute (SMI)

The Ad Hoc Committee, chaired by Mister R. Burt Gookin of the H. J. Heinz Company, was made up of eighteen well-respected executives from companies representing all areas of the grocery supply chain (Exhibit 1). The committee members were faced with the formidable task of resolving problems that required a significant understanding of both existing business practices and new technologies.

In April 1971, the Ad Hoc Committee concluded that an U.P.C. should be adopted. However, the committee also concluded that the optimization of advanced symbol scan checkout systems should not be the sole justification of the business case. While the committee focused most of the initial analysis on retail operations, it was understood that the U.P.C. would have broad applications for manufacturers and third parties as well. Therefore, the decision-making process for the length and structure of the standardized code took into consideration the desires of both the retailers and manufacturers.

A Symbol Standardization Subcommittee chaired by Mister Alan Haberman (appointed to the Ad Hoc Committee) was formed to research and evaluate alternative symbol proposals. The evaluation process, including presentations to manufacturing groups and key executives, continued through 1972 and early 1973, By March 1973, the committee was ready to issue its decision. In the end, the committee voted by secret ballot to accept the symbol proposed by IBM, the symbol still used today, because it excelled in ease of printing and error detection capability.

> The shortcomings of the other "symbol" proposals would have prevented applying the U.P.C Symbol to many items, such as soda cans, bottles, wax cartons, etc. I believe all [bar-coding] applications would still have been possible but may not have been attempted so early had the U.P.C not been such an overwhelming success and shown the world the practicality of bar coding.
>
> – George Lauter,
> designer of the U.P.C. Symbol

The U.P.C. and U.P.C. symbol had been approved. The next challenge was to roll out the U.P.C. to the industry and gain broad acceptance among both manufacturers and retailers.

OBSTACLES TO IMPLEMENTATION

Gaining agreement on a Universal Product Code and U.P.C. symbol was no doubt a success. However, the progression of scanning and the U.P.C. in the grocery industry from concept to reality was by no means an inevitable occurrence. There were questions as to whether or not the decision to move forward with the implementation of the U.P.C. made economic sense. The grocery industry's tradition of limited trust and adversarial relationships had to be overcome as well. And finally, there was additional opposition to the U.P.C. both within and outside the grocery industry, some of which was substantial.

The first consideration with regard to the adoption of the U.P.C. was whether or not the savings from the U.P.C. would offset the costs of implementation. A business case for the U.P.C. had to be prepared. McKinsey & Company had been retained by the Ad Hoc Committee to research a business case and document the economic impact on all the affected parties. Potential areas for costs and savings were broken down based on whether or not the benefits were quantifiable (hard) or indirect (soft). The committee established benchmarks for manufacturers, retailers, and distributors so that they could compute savings and costs for a "typical" organization.[5] These net benefits were totaled and presented to the Ad Hoc Committee for review.

Despite the consensus to move forward with the U.P.C., economic benefits would continue to be limited until the U.P.C. was widely accepted and implemented. In the first years after its adoption there remained a number of forces within the grocery industry opposed to the use of the U.P.C. and scanner technology that worked to slow the broadscale implementation of the U.P.C. and investment in scanning systems.

Technology was changing rapidly at the time. There were concerns voiced that it was too early to establish a standard symbol, that the estab-

[5]Ad Hoc Committee definition of a typical store – $2 million per year, 9,000 SKU's, with an average labor of $6.10 per hour.

lishment of a standard in 1973 would lock the industry into a symbol standard that would soon be technologically outdated and, in the long run, limiting on the grocery industry. These interests felt instead that, over time, market mechanisms would determine the standard for bar codes.

Furthermore, there were valid concerns within the industry that the adoption of the U.P.C. would create a bi-modal world of haves and have-nots. Even if the cost/benefit equation was favorable, would the benefits somehow be limited to only the largest manufacturers and retailers? Would the start-up costs be a prohibitive barrier to smaller retailers? Were there antitrust implications?

Outside of the industry, the fiercest opposition to the U.P.C. came from the unions. The chief selling point of the U.P.C. was increased productivity. The unions felt the U.P.C. would result in the loss of jobs and sought to impose work rules and legislation to preserve the jobs of union members. Some grocery insiders wondered if it was worth the effort to pick a fight with unions over something that may or may not work.

Consumer advocates tapping into the rising force of consumerism in the United States represented another force ·of opposition to the U.P.C. There were fringe issues from religious groups claiming "Mark of the Beast" and other groups claiming the U.P.C. was just another way of "Big Brother" keeping tabs on everyone. However, there were also very legitimate concerns, namely whether consumers could trust electronic scanning systems over individual price marking. Consumer advocates questioned if retailers could be trusted to communicate pricing information fairly to the consumers.

By tapping into the rights of consumers and using the consumer advocates as allies, unions successfully lobbied for the passage of price-marking legislation in many states. The net effect of the legislation was the reduction of potential benefits of the U.P.C., thereby lengthening the payback period for the investment in scanner technology. With the extremely high cost of capital and unstable economic environment of the late 1970s and early 1980s, a number of grocery chains decided to hold off on investing in the new technology.

Ultimately the drop in the cost of capital combined with the drop in computing costs, improvements in scanner technology, elimination of price-marking legislation, and the general strengthening of the economy as a whole fueled the increased adoption of scanners and U.P.C. technology in the 1980s.

WHY THE U.P.C. ADOPTION SUCCEEDED

June 26, 1974 marked the first time that the U.P.C. symbol was used to scan a product at a live checkout register in a real store. The fact that, twenty-five years later, the U.P.C. Symbol is taken for granted is the best evidence one can provide to demonstrate that the U.P.C. code and symbol decision was a remarkable success. To this day, the U.P.C. remains one of the most impressive examples of an entire industry coming together to set a standard and succeeding.

Why did it succeed? More specifically, how did the Ad Hoc Committee manage to get everyone in an industry with a history of combative relationships and tight margins to work together and spend billions of dollars to make the U.P.C. symbol a reality?

Consider the U.P.C. in the light of some other industry standards. The U.P.C. was not an act of law as was nutritional labeling and, therefore, mandated to come into existence. The adoption of the metric system, another big industry push in the 1970s, didn't get much further than 2-liter sodas. Why then did the U.P.C. succeed where other attempts at standardization and collaboration have failed?

In order to achieve the goal of implementing the U.P.C. symbol, consensus within the committee and buy-in from the industry were absolute requirements. Due to the history of the grocery industry, committee members knew that trust, reputation, and influence of a few individuals, while valuable assets, would not be enough by themselves to secure approval of the U.P.C. The committee members knew that any proposal they put forth would come under heavy scrutiny.

The Ad Hoc Committee determined it would be best to address the code and symbol decisions separately. The savings and benefits for the code itself were much easier to quantify and support. With the symbol decision, there was a lot of speculation regarding the costs and feasibility of scanners. As the selection of a symbol would be inherently dependent on the code approved by the industry, the code decision was addressed first. Once the industry approved moving forward with the Universal

Product Code, a separate subcommittee would begin work on the symbol decision.

There are four main reasons why the U.P.C. adoption succeeded. First, the case for the U.P.C. was focused on real opportunities, not futuristic possibilities. Second, the projected benefits were conservatively estimated so that they would be easily supported and less subject to speculation. Third, it was acknowledged that enough manufacturers and retailers had to be on board in order for the U.P.C. to achieve the critical mass necessary for implementation to succeed. Finally, the Ad Hoc Committee was made up of influential, well-respected executives from all areas of the supply chain so that all interests were represented. The members of the committee leveraged their experience, knowledge, and reputations in advocating the adoption of the U.P.C. to all levels of the supply chain to ensure critical mass would be achieved. In short, their leadership provided the critical difference between success and failure.

REAL SOLUTIONS TO REAL PROBLEMS

One of the keys to selling the grocery manufacturers, retailers, and distributors on the U.P.C. was to identify the relevant issues that the U.P.C. must address. Automated checkstands had been theorized as early as 1932. The desire to gather POS data goes back to the 1940s. Direct store delivery (DSD) as we know it today was beginning to take form in the 1960s. Primitive bar coding applications had begun to see commercial use in warehouses in the late 1960s. Finally, supply-chain collaboration was as relevant an issue in the early 1970s as it is today.

The potential impact for a standardized code on all these aspects of the grocery industry was tremendous. The committee knew that, as a result of having a standard product code, there were potential savings in the areas of checker productivity, inventory management, automated ordering, DSD control, and shrinkage – just to name a few. However, in order to get the industry on board, it was necessary to show that the costs would be sufficiently offset by savings that could be quantified.

In order to ensure the industry-wide acceptance necessary to successfully implement the U.P.C., the savings had to be substantial enough to ensure that everyone in the industry would reap the benefits. Furthermore, benefits had to be achievable in the short term. A well-developed business case for cost/benefit projections was essential to the eventual success of the U.P.C.

The Ad Hoc Committee decided that the hard savings alone had to be significant enough to justify the industry acceptance of the U.P.C. Furthermore, hard savings were more likely to be realized in the short term than would soft savings, helping to sustain momentum and demonstrate to late adopters the value of the U.P.C. Finally, it was easier to get the industry on-board using hard savings as the logic behind these savings was much easier for people in the industry to endorse. In order to avoid selling the industry on something it may not be ready to undertake, the Ad Hoc Committee was purposefully conservative on soft savings estimates allowing only twenty-five percent of any estimates to count in the business case presented to the industry.

The majority of savings presented in the business case centered on two main areas where costs could be significantly reduced: labor costs in the checkstand and the price marking of individual items. At the checkstand, the costs associated with checker productivity, training, bookkeeping, and checkout losses were the focus. With price marking, the costs associated with pricing and repricing packages proved to be a major source of potential savings, and controversy as mentioned earlier. To compute hard savings, the Ad Hoc Committee tapped its members to provide time studies and work standards to accurately cost the total savings from scanning and price marking. By keeping the savings focused, simple, and based on real data, the Ad Hoc Committee had established for itself a significant beachhead of easily justified savings from which it could attack the cost concerns of the grocery retailers, manufacturers, and distributors.

CONSERVATIVE ESTIMATES FOCUSED ON HARD SAVINGS

Based on the hard benefits alone, the Ad Hoc Committee knew that it had a business case it could sell to the industry. As such, the committee wanted to make sure that the conclusions reached in the proposal would stand up to any amount of scrutiny. However, the committee recognized that there would be numerous uses for the U.P.C. beyond simple increases in productivity.

The U.P.C. proposal could have been sold based solely on the potential for hard savings. By including soft benefits in the proposal, the committee was potentially giving opponents of the U.P.C. an angle for questioning the validity of the proposal, Conversely, the committee felt that not including soft savings would also have exposed the proposal to the premise that it was not complete and that it was too biased toward the retailer.

The soft savings from inventory management and tracking of sales were speculative, tended to benefit manufacturers, and required changes in planning processes and supply-chain relationships in order to be achieved. At the same time, it was questionable whether or not the industry would be able to implement these solutions in the near future.

The solution was to focus the proposal on hard benefits and include soft benefits, but with their contribution heavily discounted. By doing this, the Ad Hoc Committee was able to present what they felt was a complete picture of the potential savings attainable from implementation of the U.P.C. By discounting the soft savings, the potential for questioning the proposal was limited by acknowledging that the savings were, in fact, speculative. However, the soft savings did present tantalizing possibilities, especially to the manufacturing community. By presenting soft savings as such a small portion of the overall benefits, the focus of the proposal remained on the quantifiable benefits.

The committee shared these findings with a third significant group – hardware and software manufacturers. These vendors had to be convinced that a significant enough market for a then non-existent bar code would exist in order for them to justify the investment to gear up factories to produce products to support the new standard.

The goal was to convince all companies, from grocery manufacturers to hardware manufacturers to retailers, that the committee had a strong enough case to generate the (ROI) required to justify investments in equipment. The care taken to balance all sides of the business case was remarkable. Benefits projected were large enough to rally interest, return on investment yet not so grandiose as to spark skepticism.

PROJECTED BENEFITS

The benefits (savings less costs) were divided into two categories, hard benefits and soft benefits. Hard benefits were tangible and quantifiable, based on reducing costs such as labor, checkout losses, and bookkeeping. Soft benefits, also referred to as intangible benefits, were more speculative and difficult to quantify. The committee felt that it was important to lay out these ideas for operational improvements to the industry. Since the hard benefits were enough to sell the U.P.C. Symbol to the industry, the committee did not want to expose what was a solid business case to speculation. In the final proposal, the soft savings were spelled out, their value estimated, and then discounted 75 percent.

In 1972, total sales in the grocery industry were in excess of $100 billion.[6] However, the committee knew that not all grocery stores would get onboard immediately. Being conservative, the committee projected that only larger stores and chains would participate initially. The annual sales for stores projected to participate was estimated to total $15.6 billion. The net benefits (savings less costs) projected for the industry was $143 million per year (Exhibit 2), or .92 percent of sales for participating stores (Exhibit 3).

While there were significant hard and soft benefits projected, the committee was confident that the hard benefits alone were significant enough to justify acceptance of the U.P.C. business case; the soft benefits were icing on the cake. Of the $143 million, $120 million was the projected benefit considering only hard costs and savings. As such, in the event that no investments were made to pursue the projected soft benefits, the U.P.C. would result in total net benefits equal to .77 percent of sales, soft benefits, after discounting, represented approximately .15 percent of sales.

PROJECTED SAVINGS

By conducting a series of intensive time studies, the committee was able to develop models by which they could estimate productivity

---

[6]"The Grocery Industry in the U.S.A. – Choice of a Universal Product Code," *Harvard Business Review,* May 1974, p. 1.

improvements gained by using the U.P.C. symbol. Using other "reasonable" assumptions approved by the committee, estimates were developed with regards to loss prevention, primarily at the checkout counter.

The hard savings were computed for a $2,000,000 store to be $62,500 per year, or 3.13 percent of sales. Even after costs were taken into account, hard benefits by themselves were significant enough to sell the U.P.C. and symbol to the grocery industry and satisfy the two and one-half year payback requirement established by the Ad Hoc Committee.

One of the main benefits of having a Universal Product Code is that everyone in the supply chain would be working off the same set of product numbers, thus facilitating possible improvements in intercompany operations. In addition, as a result of having detailed POS data, there were indirect benefits that could be realized through improvements in store management. These five areas for potential soft savings as identified by the committee were: automatic reorder, shrink control, improved warehouse operations, improved DSD control, and inventory reduction and sales increase. In the final proposal, the soft savings were spelled out, their value estimated, and then discounted 75 percent.

Whereas all hard savings were projected for retailers, manufacturers would be able to realize a limited amount of soft savings through automated tracking of coupon redemption. All totaled, the soft savings were projected to be only 1.15 percent of sales, before being discounted, as compared to 3.13 percent for hard savings. After the 75 percent adjustment, the projected soft savings were only .29 percent of sales.

PROJECTED COSTS

Implementation of the U.P.C. required significant investments. From manufacturers down through distributors and retailers, making the U.P.C. a reality was not going to be cheap. Manufacturers were going to incur costs from changing their packaging and labels to add the U.P.C. Symbol to their products. Distributors had to invest in hardware and software in order to take advantage of the benefits made possible from having a standardized product code. Retailers had to invest not only in checkstand scanners, but also hardware and software to handle warehouse operations as well as all of the POS data they would be gathering.

Finally, equipment vendors had to design and produce field-ready hardware at competitive prices.

Since the personal computer had not been invented, the costs of mainframes prohibited having one in every store. Furthermore, the cost of storing data in the 1970s was relatively expensive. As a result, it was necessary to transmit POS data up to a central mainframe on a regular basis. While the Internet did technically exist in 1974, there was no World-wide Web as we know it today, so all of the data was transmitted over leased lines at very slow speeds, thus further increasing the costs for implementing the U.P.C. And because there were no fax machines, inter-company data exchange was best done with difficult to read computer tapes or hard copy printouts.

Having a Universal Product Code also required assigning someone to manage it. While the creation of a central body, the aforementioned UCC, was a foregone conclusion, the responsibilities of such a body needed to be determined. At one point, the idea of having the UCC manage every code was discussed, but then dismissed as being cost prohibitive. In the end, it was determined that the UCC would manage the manufacturer codes and each manufacturer would be allotted a fixed amount of numbers to assign to their products as they saw fit.

All totaled, hard costs were projected to be 2.36 percent of sales. Costs related to soft benefits were projected to be .55 percent of sales, .14 percent after discounting. Combined with the hard and soft savings projected, 3.13 percent and .29 percent of sales respectively, net projected benefits from the U.P.C. were .77 percent of sales for hard benefits and .15 percent of sales for soft benefits.

THE CRITICAL MASS PROBLEM

The potential savings from the U.P.C. did not accrue across the supply chain in proportion with costs to be incurred. Projections were that, in the beginning, tangible benefits would be realized primarily by retailers while the benefits for manufacturers were practically non-existent; the grocery manufacturers as a group actually stood to lose money.

The prediction was that the savings would eventually trickle up through the supply chain to the manufacturers. Unfortunately, "Reaganomics" would not become part of the American language for another decade and the promise of eventual benefits did not sell as well in 1970 as it might have in the 1980s. Conversely, without enough manufacturers participating, the savings for retailers would be significantly less than predicted.

The grocery industry had to be sold on the U.P.C. and scanning. Manufacturers needed to be convinced that a significant segment of the retail industry would adopt scanning technology before they were willing to incur the costs associated with printing and administering the U.P.C. for every package they produced. Retailers understood that the investment in scanners would only be worthwhile if a high percentage of manufacturers agreed to source mark their products. Hardware vendors would have to be reasonably sure of potential sales volumes before they would commit research and development dollars to developing hardware technology based on the U.P.C. symbol.

The situation represented a "chicken and egg" problem; neither manufacturers, nor retailers, nor hardware vendors would be willing to make the necessary investments unless they were sure of participation by the others. Achieving a "critical mass" was necessary in order to realize the potential benefit of the U.P.C. In the cost-benefit analysis presented to the committee, the critical mass projected was that 75 percent of items would be source marked and that a significant number of grocery stores would implement scanner technology. The Ad Hoc Committee viewed the critical mass issue as the most important obstacle to implementation and took active steps to build their case and then communicate it throughout the industry.

LEADERSHIP FROM THE AD HOC COMMITTEE

The implementation of the U.P.C. was a significant undertaking for the whole industry. Fundamental changes in business processes were necessary. One of the keys to any successful change management initiative is the leadership of senior management in the change process. With the U.P.C. symbol initiative, the Ad Hoc Committee was the management team for the grocery industry. The Ad Hoc Committee members managed the process, made decisions, provided leadership, used publications to sustain momentum, and kept lines of communication open between the Ad Hoc Committee and the rest of the industry.

Though the problems confronting the members of the Ad Hoc Committee were technically complex, all of them were generalists. They were basically chief executives and prominent and well known in the trade . . . Resolution of the problems they faced needed an ability to compromise. . . . They bring in or consult with technical guys, which they did, but their generalist orientation was a key factor.

    – An industry insider commenting on the choice of the Ad Hoc Committee[7]

The Ad Hoc Committee consisted primarily of presidents, vice-presidents, and C.E.O.s. Members were selected from manufacturers, distributors, and retailers to insure that the interests of all parts of the grocery supply chain were represented. In addition to being corporate executives, the individuals selected for the committee had significant knowledge, respect, and influence within the entire industry. Finally, to insure participation of the members, attendance at meetings was mandatory. Only official members could vote; voting in absentia or delegation of voting responsibility was not allowed. Without mandatory participation to industry executives at this level, the speed with which both decisions and compromises could be made would have been greatly constrained, thereby inhibiting the overall effectiveness and efficiency of the initiative.

Intense scrutiny with regard to costs, scanners, and technological feasibility awaited any proposal regarding a U.P.C. Symbol. As such, the Committee felt that presenting the Code and Symbol together would be too complex and theoretical, thereby causing the failure of the U.P.C. initiative.

Within the Ad Hoc Committee, consensus to the code decision was complicated by the fact that the even small changes with regard to length, structure, and compatibility of the U.P.C. dramatically altered the distribution of savings and costs in the supply chain. While it was natural for each member of the Ad Hoc Committee to look out for their

[7]"The Grocery Industry in the USA – Choice of a Universal Product Code," *Harvard Business Review,* May 1974, p. 4.

own best interests, reaching a consensus on these issues was the critical step along the way to securing the necessary participation of all levels in the supply chain. The Ad Hoc Committee accepted the possibility that a sub-optimal standard might be necessary in order to ensure that no portion of the supply chain bore a disproportionate burden of the implementation costs. Without the wisdom and influence of the Committee members selected, many of these compromises would not have been made, decisions would have been postponed, and the U.P.C. initiative would have gone the way of other failed attempts to establish a standardized product code.

In an effort to gain the critical mass of support needed for success, Ad Hoc Committee members took great pains, including time away from their own businesses, to tour the country pitching the case for the establishment of a U.P.C. It is worth noting that they were able to win widespread support throughout the industry solely on the basis of the business case and their own reputations. For example, between March and May of 1971, Larry Russell and Tom Wilson of McKinsey, along with others in the committee, made over 250 presentations to industry representatives. As one outside observer commented:

> The idea was to create a suitable climate, a climate of being with the "in thing." The idea was to gain the commitment of key trade group presidents, and chief executives of 50–60 key retailers and manufacturers. If they stood behind the U.P.C. in principle, we knew it would stick. Their commitment would make others follow suit. It was tricky, but it worked.[8]

After the U.P.C. was approved, the Ad Hoc Committee sustained momentum and interest in the initiative by communicating there progress through trade publications such as *Progressive Grocer*. By keeping the industry abreast of developments and time lines, the committee was able to address interests in the grocery industry that were not represented on the committee. In addition, the Ad Hoc Committee used articles

[8]"The Grocery Industry in the U.S.A. – Choice of a Universal Product Code," *Harvard Business Review*, May 1974, p. 19.

in these publications to tout the potential uses of the U.P.C., point-of-sale (POS) data, and scanners in order to maintain the level of enthusiasm in the grocery industry.

Selling the U.P.C. to the industry, facilitating consensus, securing the participation necessary for critical mass, and maintaining momentum represent some of the most significant accomplishments for the Ad Hoc Committee. The leadership exhibited by the Ad Hoc Committee in bringing the industry together to reach consensus and keep the industry together long enough to implement the U.P.C. and U.P.C. symbol is, to many people, as remarkable all achievement as the success of the U.P.C. symbol itself.

25 YEARS LATER . . . THE ACTUAL RESULTS

PricewaterhouseCoopers has reviewed all of the original business case documents and validated their assumptions against productivity standards and operating efficiencies that have actually been achieved. System and hardware costs were compared to the original estimates. Finally, economic factors (i.e., interest rates and inflation) and actual grocery industry and alternative channels were used to recompute the projected benefits and restate them in 1997 dollars.[9]

Has the U.P.C. achieved the benefits predicted in the 1974 business case? The answer to this question is both yes and no. Purely from the perspective of the grocery industry, given today's productivity, wages, and technology, the "hard" annual benefits (hard savings less costs) from the U.P.C. symbol today are estimated at approximately 2.8 percent of sales, or more than 3.5 times what was originally projected (Exhibit 4). Whereas the original estimates were based on approximately 15 percent of store volume implementing the use of scanning, over 87 percent of all sales in the grocery industry are U.P.C. scanned. Adjusting for inflation, the projected hard benefits of $120 million per year in 75 are equivalent to $307 million per year in 1997 (Exhibit 5).[10] In 1997, hard savings real-

[9]Used 1997 as complete 1998 information not available at the time of publication.
[10]Benefits realized have been estimated by taking the same methodology used by McKinsey & Co. in 1973 and applying the methodology to the grocery industry in 1997.

ized across the grocery industry were in excess of $8 billion, more than 26 times the hard savings projected in dollar terms!

However, the view of PricewaterhouseCoopers is that the majority of savings that could have been realized still remain to be captured by those participants with the imagination to exploit the value of U.P.C. data more collaboratively. Later we will develop an analysis of the areas of potential savings that fall primarily into what the committee termed soft benefits. We conservatively estimate these benefits to be in excess of $15.25 billion or five percent of industry revenues.

HARD SAVINGS REALIZED

Automated checkstands have enabled the use of more part-time labor for checkout, thereby keeping wages down. Stores today are even installing self-scanning checkout systems, helping to further reduce labor costs. The amount of time it takes to train an individual checker has dropped dramatically, more than compensating for increased training costs resulting from having to train more part-time cashiers. And the U.P.C. has helped to dramatically reduce checkout losses, particularly misrings, sweethearting, and improper handling of coupons.

Increases in productivity and reduction in wages have helped to push the benefits from the U.P.C. past original projections. However, the hard savings projected by the committee on a per item basis have remained pretty much in line with the hard savings actually realized. The primary difference between the projected net benefits and the benefits being realized today is twofold: first, the greater scope of U.P.C. scanning; and second, the way costs have been dramatically reduced over the past twenty-five years, specifically the costs of scanners, computers, and other technology.

The size of the grocery industry today is around $337 billion in sales, approximately 87 percent of which is U.P.C. scanned. The discount, drug, convenience, club, and super center channels combine for $334 billion in annual sales with an estimated $248 billion, or 74 percent, U.P.C. scanned (Exhibit 6). Therefore, hard dollars saved due to the U.P.C. are approximately $6 billion *outside* the grocery industry. Combined with the $8.1 billion in hard benefits from the grocery industry, the U.P.C. is generating in excess of $14 billion in hard benefits per year, even after adjusting for inflation, the hard benefits are more than forty-five times the $120 million per year originally projected.

Adjusted for inflation, the cost per checklane for hardware (scanner, register, and maintenance) has dropped over 85 percent between 1974 and 1999. This does not include the costs associated with back-end computers, mainframes, data transmission, and networking which have dropped even more dramatically. As a result, PricewaterhouseCoopers estimates the actual costs to be only 0.70 percent of sales compared to the 2.36 percent originally estimated.

Based on the actual hard costs and savings, the U.P.C. has been a tremendous success as compared to the business case presented to the industry twenty-five years ago. However, having been the focus of so much optimization in the past twenty-five years, one has to wonder how much more can saved in this area. To gauge the impact of the U.P.C. on the future of the food industry, we must shift our focus to the softer side of the U.P.C. proposal.

SOFT SAVINGS PARTIALLY ACHIEVED

While the industry was successful in fully implementing the U.P.C. Symbol and extracting the hard benefits that were predicted, the performance of the industry with regard to realizing the soft benefits projected has been, at best, satisfactory.

In the original U.P.C. proposal, the five areas identified as areas from which soft savings could be extracted were: automatic reorder, shrink control, improved warehouse operations, improved DSD control, and inventory reduction and sales increase. The premise was that, by cooperating with one another and sharing POS data, grocery retailers and manufacturers could save money. Again, since the savings from implementing these programs were speculative, the committee heavily discounted the projected benefits. These "soft" savings were estimated at 0.60 percent of sales and discounted to only 0.15 percent in the Ad Hoc Committee's business case. Various industry studies would suggest that DSD receiving improvements, when properly split between manufacturers, along with shrink control from eliminating under-rings will more than exceed the $440 million in today's dollars – that was predicted in the original business case – in soft savings. In fact, various industry studies put the value from shrink and DSD control above the 0.6 percent of revenue that was estimated prior to any discounting by the committee, resulting in annual soft benefits approaching $1.8 billion.

Yet several areas of "soft" U.P.C. benefits identified in 1974 remain untapped and others, not originally identified, have yet to be fully exploited. The original McKinsey business case singled out automatic reorder, automation of warehouse operations, along with increased sales and reduced inventories resulting from the adoption of the U.P.C. Twenty-five years later, automatic reordering, or computer-aided ordering (CAO) as it is currently referred to, has not gone beyond pilot testing in a few chains. Similarly, warehouse automation has gone a different route with EDI and UCS communications standards making use of the U.P.C. nomenclature, but not the bar code.

The case for the use of the U.P.C. data to better plan and manage inventory and build revenues is also problematic. U.P.C. tracking data has become the gold standard for evaluating brand and category volumes, trends, and market shares. Information Resources Incorporated (IRI) and A.C. Nielsen dominate this sector. In addition, a number of smaller companies have built businesses around decision support or demand creation activities (i.e. electronic coupons, promotion analysis tools, household consumption panels, and micro-market demographic analysis, to name a few). Taken together, PricewaterhouseCoopers estimates these firms combined revenues from U.P.C. data at just under $850 million in 1998. Using the revenue from these firms as a proxy, the value of U.P.C. tracking data for decision support in better managing inventory to costs and increasing revenues equates to 0.29 percent of industry sales.

Significant savings have also been realized through more efficient replenishment practices in the areas of advance ship notices (ASNs), continuous replenishment forecasting, and other initiatives that make use of U.P.C. data. According to a report by Ernst & Young, better demand forecasting, reduction of inefficiencies, and other improvements in logistics have already generated savings on the order of 15 percent to 35 percent of the warehouse, transportation, and order processing costs for consumer packaged goods (CPG) companies, which are estimated to average about ten percent of sales. PricewaterhouseCoopers' analysis of the total impact of the U.P.C., in the creation of "soft" benefits is therefore 0.60 percent + 0.29 percent + 2.00 percent, or 2.89 percent of industry revenues (Exhibit 7). This total is nineteen times what was originally forecast by the Ad Hoc Committee for "soft" benefits and equates to $8.5 billion in annual savings for the grocery industry.

THE UNTAPPED POTENTIAL OF THE U.P.C.

The irony of reporting how the success of the U.P.C. effort has exceeded its original estimates is not in what was achieved, but in how much more might have been achieved had the grocery industry been able to collaborate more effectively.

While discounting the potential "soft" benefits helped to reduce the risk that the U.P.C. proposal would be blocked, others in the industry believed that the Ad Hoc Committee discounted the potential soft savings too dramatically. When the U.P.C. was implemented, the potential soft savings fell by the wayside and were not aggressively pursued by manufacturers and retailers in the grocery industry. The Ad Hoc Committee has been accused of creating a self-fulfilling prophecy. The reaction of committee members remains that they were correct and that the industry was simply not ready to make the changes necessary to generate the soft savings projected. Regardless, the use of POS data for automatic reorder, shrink control, and inventory reduction and consumer tracking was ignored in the grocery industry for almost twenty years.

With the adoption of the U.P.C., the grocery industry was, for a brief moment, the leader in technology and supply chain management. Its failure to go further left inefficiencies in the grocery industry supply chain, allowing other distribution channels to steal market share. In effect, these other channels concentrated on the "soft" benefits by removing inefficiencies from their supply chains to create a cost advantage over traditional grocery stores and establish inroads into the food distribution business. A key theme that runs through these efficiencies is the sharing of U.P.C. data and the collaboration among trading partners to plan and execute lower cost processes.

EFFICIENT CONSUMER RESPONSE –
A CLARION CALL UNHEEDED

In mid-1992, largely in response to inroads made by discount stores into the food industry, industry leaders created a "joint-industry task force." The task force was charged with examining the grocery supply chain and its trade practices to identify potential opportunities for changes in practices or in technology that would make the supply chain more competitive."[11] Bringing with it the potential for $30 billion in annual savings plus 40 percent lower inventories for the industry, the Efficient Consumer Response movement was officially born in 1993.

> In recent years, a growing number of grocery retailers, distributors, suppliers, and brokers have become increasingly concerned that the grocery is losing its competitive edge. Productivity growth in food retailing over the last twenty years has fallen behind other retail channels. These other channels have also caught up with, and in some cases surpassed, the grocery industry's technological lead in electronic data interchange and bar coded product identification[12]

The potential savings for ECR, approximately 10 percent of industry sales, were broken down into five categories in the 1997 ECR industry benchmarking survey.[13] The categories are efficient replenishment, category management, efficient promotion, efficient assortment, and efficient product introduction. While the terms had changed, the basic concept remained the same as in 1974, there are significant amounts of savings to be realized by sharing data and working together to optimize the total cost in the supply chain.

---

[11]"Efficient Consumer Response, Enhancing Consumer Value in the Grocery Industry," Kurt Salmon Associates, Inc., January 1993, foreword.
[12]Ibid.
[13]"1997 ECR Industry Benchmarking Survey," Kurt Salmon Associates, Inc., 1998, executive summary.

... bar-coding and EDI are commonly referred to as the "enabling technologies" as they allow business partners to move information and product more rapidly and at lower overall cost. In turn, this taster movement of information and product enables the retailer and the manufacturer to better anticipate, detect, and respond to consumers' needs, thereby better satistfying the customer and capturing market share from slower competitors.[14]

While EDI has been the most widely implemented component of supply chain management in the grocery industry, EDI has mainly been used as a means of communicating purchase orders and invoice transaction sets. In most instances, EDI is not being used as an enabling technology. To date, the use of POS data for improved demand management and the sharing of POS data for analysis purposes has been limited.

EFFICIENT REPLENISHMENT VIA IMPROVED COLLABORATION

Citing "modern technology" and the "development of advanced information systems" as essential to realizing the potential benefits of ECR, a report by Ernst & Young to the ECR operating committee identified a series of enablers for the pursuit of further supply chain savings: EDI, POS scanning, activity based costing (ABC), computer-assisted ordering, flow-through distribution, and continuous replenishment. Implicit in each practice and taken for granted today is the use of U.P.C. data. Increased efficiency in data gathering combined with improvements in electronic communications has resulted in the implementation of some supply chain efficiencies. However, the implementation of ECR and efficient replenishment best practices has lagged behind industry expectations. In the 1997 ECR benchmarking survey, the industry leaders had reached full ECR compliance in only one third of "key ECR practices." The most widely implemented ECR practices – EDI purchase orders

---

[14]"Efficient Consumer Response, Enhancing Consumer Value in the Grocery Industry," Kurt Salmon Associates, Inc., January 1993, p. 20.

and invoices – have been around in the industry since before 1993. According to one industry expert, all the savings that have been achieved thus far do not equal the amount of savings that still remains on the table. Comparing several surveys of results to date, PricewaterhouseCoopers believes that at least another $6 to $7 billion remains to be captured if the potential improvements in efficient replenishment were fully realized.

When initially proposed, ECR, like the U.P.C., met with its share of criticism. The difficulty some are facing with implementation has only helped to fuel the fire of critics. One criticism is that the prescribed ECR best practices address the symptoms, not the root causes of supply chain inefficiency. But perhaps the real issue is the failure of collaboration to advance existing supply chain practices.

In October of last year, the cover of *Progressive Grocer* touted the new age of collaboration. While companies are working together more cooperatively than in the past, the main reason provided for the collaboration was the financial rewards that could be reaped from cooperation. Conversely, in *Progressive Grocer's Sixty-Fifth Annual Report of the Grocery Industry* released in April 1998, the results of a survey on trade relations were published. The results of the survey, which focused on executives, indicated that the footing upon which the age of collaboration stood was not very stable. Trust levels were mediocre at best. Furthermore, a significant percentage of respondents felt trade relations had not improved over the past five years. Finally, well over 60 percent of respondents felt that power in the industry was shifting, the vast majority felt that power was shifting away from them.

One area of replenishment that can be greatly improved through increased collaboration is forecasting. By sharing information related to sales data, promotions, and sales forecasts, the need for forecasting in the supply chain can be greatly reduced. For example, if a store knows how much of a product it is planning to purchase over the next week or month, the store can inform the distributor who in turns informs the manufacturer. By sharing this information, the distributor does not have to forecast what the store will order and the manufacturer knows how much to produce for the distributor and both can more accurately schedule transportation. The end result is that the distributor and manufacturer do not have to spend time forecasting and "safety stocks" can be reduced.

The need for sales forecasts based on historical U.P.C. data will never be eliminated. But it can be significantly improved. One way in which forecasting accuracy can be improved is by compressing lead times. Data availability is becoming more real-time. By increasing the frequency of data transmissions upstream from the POS to the distributor and manufacturer, the planning horizons for the entire supply chain can be improved thereby further reducing the need for buffer inventories in the supply chain.

As the other retail channels have demonstrated, the savings are real and they were there for the taking. Improving information systems, data integration, and upgrading facilities takes time and patience. Changing corporate cultures, buyer/seller behavior, and traditional channel relationships requires total commitment from all parties. "Cooperation, not competition" is easy to say; living it is not. In the meantime, super centers, discount stores, and warehouse clubs continue to steal share of wallet and share of stomach from the grocery channel because their business model enjoys lower distribution costs.

EFFICIENT NEW PRODUCT INTRODUCTION

Revenue growth from developing and marketing new products to meet the consumers' need for convenience, variety, or value should be a high priority for the industry. Every year, 20,000 new U.P.C.s hit the grocery shelves; only 6 percent, approximately 1,200, of the 20,000 represent new brands, line extensions, or totally new products. According to research conducted by Ernst & Young, approximately two-thirds of these fail.[15] Despite the vast amounts of potential data to track which new products entered the market and failed, manufacturers and retailers have not made significant progress on improving the results of this process.

The cost of failure is high. Studies have estimated the manufacturer cost to launch a new line extension or new brand at between $10 million and $25 million per launch. Grocery retailers are estimated to spend nearly $1 million per store on new products that eventually fail.[16] Even allowing for slotting allowances, which may not actually reflect the retail-

---

[15]Ernst & Young, New Product Introduction, ECR Conference, Atlanta, February 1999.
[16]*Frozen Food Digest,* July 1, 1997.

ers out-of-pocket costs, PricewaterhouseCoopers estimates the annual industry-wide cost for the two-thirds of all products that fail at $25 to $30 billion. The 1997 ECR benchmark survey estimates that less than 15 percent of manufacturers have begun to implement strategies and practices aimed at improving the new product introduction process.

CATEGORY MANAGEMENT

While the concept of category management would be impossible without U.P.C. data to assess category performance and evaluate alternative strategies, the existence of the data has not unlocked the collaboration between suppliers and distributors needed to generate greater revenues and lower costs by better meeting consumer demand. In this "New Age" of ECR, grocery retailers, wholesalers, and manufacturers need to work together to reverse the trend of market share erosion for the grocery industry. To this end, industry leaders are working to develop information technology infrastructures to facilitate the capture and analysis of data.

When the U.P.C. was first implemented, computers were much more expensive than they are today. In addition, the computers at the time were very limited in their capabilities to perform data analysis. In the past twenty-five years, the costs of computers and data transmission have dropped exponentially. In addition to getting cheaper, the technology has gotten better and easier to use. The result is that it is easier to get access to more sales information for more products closer to real-time than ever before.

Due to ease of use and improvements in software development, data analysis has evolved from reading computer output reports to online analysis of today's sales data. Per IRI's 1997 annual report, in the mid-1980s, manual audits provided approximately 180,000 data points per category monitored. By the early 1990s, scanning had increased the amount of data to 487 million data points. In 1997, a category report could contain 2.25 billion pieces of data. The result is that there are opportunities in the application and analysis of data available today that were unheard of just a few years ago.

Unlike the other areas of ECR and the original case for the U.P.C., the business case for category management remains elusive and undocumented. In principle, determining a role for each category and linking the assortment, space, price, and promotion tactics into an integrated plan to meet consumer needs has an appealing logic. Despite a number of pilot projects supporting this claim, the sentiment to invest heavily in category management data, tools, and people is far from strong. Again, from the 1997 ECR benchmark survey, less than a third of warehouse manufacturers had strong category management programs in place. According to Winston Weber & Associates, Inc., while "90 percent of retailers say they are at various stages of implementation, only a few of them are doing it right."[17]

Whether all the effort will create incremental demand or simply shift market share among retailers in the market remains a debatable issue. As in 1971, when costs, in this case the cost of being the category captain, are not accrued in proportion to benefits then collaboration is difficult. Today, many manufacturers are still trying to figure out the business case in terms of the net benefits to their brands that result from the effort put forward in support of category management.

EFFICIENT TRADE PROMOTION

"If you are dumb enough to give me the money, I'm dumb enough to take it." – V.P. Marketing, major grocery chain

The impact of monies transferred from manufacturers to retailers for a temporary price reduction has long been recognized for its negative impact on overall operating efficiencies. While admittedly serving a good purpose in creating consumer excitement and stimulating trial of new brands or packages, trade deals have long been identified with promoting inefficiencies all along the supply chain. Brand groups deplore the erosion of price integrity, logistics. Manufacturing planners deplore the inventory surges that must be accommodated. Retailers too frequently either divert product or simply fail to pass through a significant portion of the deal to the consumer. Andersen Consulting recently estimated trade spending dollars at $20–$25 billion to "influence" retailer merchan-

---

[17]"The Future of Category Management," Winston Weber & Associates, *http://www.winstonweber.com/fcm.htm*

dising activities and asserted that much of this spending was unprofitable for the manufacturer.[18]

Despite the ECR efforts to highlight the problem, little has been accomplished. Few CPG companies have built the tools to gather and then track trade spending results. The 1997 ECR survey indicated that less than 20 percent of the efficient promotion practices had been implemented. At the 1999 ECR conference, the pessimism was even greater.

> "We haven't begun to come to grips with deal funding. Warehouse space is cheap compared to the deal funds available."
> – ECR Executive Panel, ECR Conference, Atlanta,
> February 1999

Clearly the industry has not found the key to unlock collaboration and data sharing to go after this $20 billion opportunity despite the existence of the U.P.C. data that provides a starting point for tracking and evaluation of trade spending. Manufacturers remain for the most part unable to determine which events build the value of their brands and which events simply push cases through the system.

FOCUSING ON THE CONSUMER

> Consumers, not distributors are now controlling what is being bought and sold in America's supermarkets and other food emporiums.[19]

U.P.C. reporting, until recently, could only extend supply chain visibility down the supply chain to the checkout and as far back up the chain as the willingness to collaborate and share data could be carried. The advent of frequent shopper programs a few years ago has now moved the reach of the U.P.C. past the cash register and into the home of the consumer.

Until recently, decision making was based on tracking total sales or sales by market using U.P.C. Whether a purchase was made by a loyal

---

[18]"Trade Spending Dilemma," Andersen Consulting, 1997.
[19]Chain Store Age State of the Industry Report, August 1997.

consumer or a cherry picker, whether a consumer promotion simply front-loaded a heavy user who would have bought anyway, or whether a trial was created with a new consumer was unknown.

Perhaps the most egregious practice in this area was couponing. In the United States, every year manufacturers mail the equivalent of over 2,000 coupons to every man, woman, and child in the country. Less than 2 percent are ever redeemed and conventional wisdom suggested that all this $10–$12 billion in spending achieved was to give loyal, heavy users a discount for buying what they would have bought anyway.

Now, the use of frequent shopper data promises to change everything. According to research conducted by PricewaterhouseCoopers, the behavior of 30–40 percent of all households account for 80+% of brand, category, and store volumes. By allowing U.P.C. purchase data to be identified with the purchase history of specific households, the impact of coupons, trade deals, and new product spending can be measured directly. The value of assortment and space management decisions in a category management program no longer has to be judged at the store level but can be measured against the key households that really matter.

The willingness of retailers and manufacturer to collaborate, once again as with the U.P.C., represents the key to realizing the true potential of frequent shopper data. Data warehouses are being billed today as the key to successfully establishing enduring strategic advantages. The amount of data collected today, the speed at which information is analyzed, and improvements being made in data mining tools are enabling those manufacturers and retailers with the capability to collaborate to dramatically redefine how they compete for the loyalty of the consumer.

Still, manufacturers and retailers have a poor track record when it comes to sharing data. Since consumers are ultimately driving demand, the grocery industry must come to recognize that understanding the consumer is critical to success. PricewaterhouseCoopers' analysis of frequent shopper data suggests that both manufacturers and retailers have a lot to learn about the topic of consumer loyalty. Levels of brand loyalty are far lower than generally believed based on market share data. A recent study by IRI indicated that people with the largest per month grocery expenditures spend, on average, less than 50 percent in any single store.

In principle, the superior consumer focus inherent in frequent shopper programs will not only replace the $10–$12 billion in coupons, but it will redefine the business case for trade promotion and category management as well. By moving the value of U.P.C. data beyond point of sale and into the home of the consumer, it represents the ultimate in the realization of "soft benefits."

SUMMARY

In 1997, one percent of people said that they do not shop in supermarkets. By itself, this figure might be considered by some as insignificant. However, consider that this represents the first time since consumers were polled that the figure for consumers who shop in supermarkets was not 100 percent. In addition, the percentage of consumers shopping in other channels rose from 40 percent to 49 percent, thereby reinforcing the picture of increased competition. Perhaps more compelling is that in 1995, for the first time ever, consumers spent more on food outside the grocery channel than within the channel. With market share and customer preference being eroded by discount stores, warehouse clubs, and other channels, it is clear that the grocery industry is no longer simply competing with itself.

We have traced the history of the U.P.C. and its impact on the industry. Realized hard savings of 2.76 percent of revenues or $8.1 billion and realized soft savings of 2.89 percent of revenues or $8.9 billion compared to an original business case of .92 percent and $367 million demonstrate that the U.P.C. has been and continues to be a huge success by any standard. But what of tomorrow? As an industry, countless hours are being invested in pursuing the tenets set forth in the ECR best practices. Yet five years after its initiation, the dialog is all about simplifying the focus (Real Solutions to Real Problems?), providing a compelling business case to spur action (Conservative Estimates Focused on Hard Savings?), and much discussion regarding the need for more collaboration in new ways of working together (Leadership?). As the great philosopher, Yogi Berra, once said, "It's déjà vu all over again."

It would seem that for the grocery industry to go forward, it should perhaps look once more at the lessons from the original U.P.C. effort.

When the benefits of change are not the same for manufacturers and retailers, when the benefits of change depend upon the number of players that agree to a standard approach, when the range of benefits possible is broad and complex, as is the case in each of the ECR initiatives, then the way forward should embody the key lessons from the U.P.C.

PricewaterhouseCoopers' perspective is that while the benefits that the U.P.C. has generated are large, the opportunity going forward is even greater. Consider the case facts regarding the potential benefits yet to be captured: efficient replenishment $6–7 billion, efficient new product introduction $25–30 billion, efficient trade promotion $20–25 billion; and efficient consumer promotions $10–12 billion. Furthermore, the business cases for category management or frequent shopper have not even been captured. From an identified total of over $60 billion in the grocery industry alone, an improvement of 25 percent across the board would produce benefits of $15.25 billion or 5.2 percent of industry revenues, almost equivalent to the overall savings the grocery industry is currently achieving through the utilization of the U.P.C. Perhaps more importantly, capturing efficiencies on this scale along with the ability to better focus on the consumer would go a long way to redressing the cost disadvantages of the grocery channel compared to its major rivals. We believe that as an industry, the focus, the fact base, and the need for leadership are all essential to moving the ECR initiative into a higher gear.

Exhibit 1: The Ad Hoc Committee

NAME	COMPANY – 1971	POSITION HELD	ACTIVITY
Members:			
Robert O. Aders	Kroger Company	Chairman of the Board	Supermarket Chain
Gordon Ellis	Interstate Brands Corp.	Executive Vice President	Manufacturer
R. B. Gookin, *Chairman*	H. J. Heinz Company	President	Manufacturer
William Kane	Great Atlantic & Pacific Tea Company	Chairman	Supermarket Chain
Arthur Larkin, Jr.	General Foods Corp.	President	Manufacturer
Donald Lloyd	Associated Food Stores	President	Cooperative
Gavin MacBain	Bristol-Myers	Chairman	Manufacturer
James P. MacFarland	General Mills, Inc.	Chairman of the Board	Manufacturer
Earl Madsen	Madsen Enterprises, Inc.	President	Independent
James T. Wyman	Super Value Stores, Inc.	Chairman, Finance Committee	Supermarket Chain
Advisors:			
Frederick Butler	Bristol-Myers	Vice President	Manufacturer
John F. Hayes	H. J. Heinz Company	General Manager Marketing	Manufacturer
Thomas P. Nelson	General Mills, Inc.	Vice President	Manufacturer
Dean Potts	General Atlantic & Pacific Tea Company	Controller	Supermarket Chain
Robert A. Stringer	General Foods Corp.	Vice President	Manufacturer
Jack Strubbe	Kroger Company	Vice President	Supermarket Chain

Exhibit 2: Original Business Case — (1975 dollars)*

	Quantifiable	Intangible	
SAVINGS	(Hard)	(Soft)	Total
Grocer/Retailer	488	173	
Grocery manufacturers		6	
Code management function			
Subtotal	488	179	
Discount factor	_____	0.25	_____
TOTAL SAVINGS	488	45	533

	Quantifiable	Intangible	
Costs	(Hard)	(Soft)	Total
Grocer/Retailer	332	86	
Grocery manufacturers	30		
Code management function	6		
Subtotal	368	86	
Discount factor	_____	0.25	_____
TOTAL COSTS	368	22	390
NET BENEFIT	120	23	143

*Original business case. All amounts have been discounted back to 1975 dollars. Dollars in millions.
Notes: 1975 dollars; 7,800 stores; Labor = $6.10/Hour; Annual sales per store = $2,000,000

Exhibit 3: Original Business Case – As percent of Sales*

	Quantifiable	Intangible	
SAVINGS	(Hard)	(Soft)	Total
Grocer/Retailer	3.13	1.11	
Grocery manufacturers		.04	
Code management function			
Subtotal	3.13	1.15	
Discount factor		0.25	
	____	____	____
TOTAL SAVINGS	3.13%	.29%	3.42%
	Quantifiable	Intangible	
COSTS	(Hard)	(Soft)	Total
Grocer/Retailer	2.13	.55	
Grocery manufacturers	.19		
Code management function	.04		
Subtotal	2.36	.55	
Discount factor		0.25	
	____	____	____
TOTAL COSTS	2.36%	.14%	2.50%
NET BENEFIT	.77%	.15%	.92%

*Original business case represented as a percentage of sales. Total U.P.C. sales projected to be $15.6 billion dollars based on number of stores projected to participate in the original business case.

Notes: 7,800 stores; Labor = $6.10/Hour; Annual sales per store = $2,000,000

Exhibit 4: Business Case Updated to Reflect 1997 Productivity*

| | Original Business Case | | | Updated for 1997 | | |
	Quantifiable	Intangible		Quantifiable	Intangible	
SAVINGS	(Hard)	(Soft)	Total	(Hard)	(Soft**)	Total
Grocer/Retailer	488	173		539		
Grocery manufacturers			6			
Code management function						
Subtotal	488	179		539		
Discount factor		0.25				
TOTAL SAVINGS	488	45	533	539	537	1076

	Quantifiable	Intangible		Quantifiable	Intangible	
SAVINGS	(Hard)	(Soft)	Total	(Hard)	(Soft†)	Total
Grocer/Retailer	332	86		93	86	
Grocery manufacturers	30			10		
Code management function	6			6		
Subtotal	368	86		109	86	
Discount factor		0.25				
TOTAL COSTS	368	22	390	109	86	195
NET BENEFIT	120	23	143	430	451	881

*Original business case compared with business case if it were presented in 1997 adjusted to reflect 1997 wages, productivity, and costs. All amounts have been discounted back to 1975 dollars. Dollars are in millions.
Notes: 1975 dollars; 7,800 stores; Annual sales per store = 2,000,000

Benefits realized have been estimated by taking the same methodology used by McKinsey & Co. in 1973 and applying the methodology to the grocery industry in 1997.

Soft benefits not separated out by retailer/manufacturer. Savings based on benefits + costs. Net benefit has been 2.89 percent of sales (Exhibit 6). $15.6 billion* 2.89 percent = $451 million.

Exhibit 5: Original Business Case vs. Updated Business Case*

| | Original Business Case | | | Updated for 1997* | | |
	Quantifiable	Intangible		Quantifiable	Intangible	
SAVINGS	(Hard)	(Soft)	Total	(Hard)	(Soft)	Total
Grocer/Retailer	1,250	443		1,380		
Grocery manufacturers		15				
Code management function						
Subtotal	1,250	458		1,380		
Discount factor		0.25				
TOTAL SAVINGS	1,250	115	1,365	1,380	1,375	2,755
	Quantifiable	Intangible		Quantifiable	Intangible	
COSTS	(Hard)	(Soft)	Total	(Hard)	(Soft**)	Total
Grocer/Retailer	850	220		238	220	
Grocery manufacturers	77			26		
Code management function	15			15		
Subtotal	942	220		279	220	
Discount factor		0.25				
TOTAL COSTS	942	55	997	279	220	499
NET BENEFIT	307	60	367	1,101	1,155	2,256

*Exhibit 4 updated to 1997 dollars. Original case compared with business case if it were presented in 1997 adjusted to reflect 1997 wages, productivity, and costs. All amounts have been adjusted forward to reflect 1997 dollars. Dollars are in millions.
Notes: 1997 dollars; 7,800 stores; Total sales = $40 billion (7,800 stores* $2 million/store* CPI food-at-home adjustment factor); CPI food at home index adjustment factor = 2.56047

Benefits realized have been estimated by taking the same methodology used by McKinsey & Co. in 1973 and applying the methodology to the grocery industry in 1997.

Soft benefits not separated out by retailer/manufacturer. Savings based on Benefits + Costs. Net benefit has been 2.89% of sales (Exhibit 6). $15.6 billion* 2.89% = $451 million.

Exhibit 6: Grocery Sales by Retail Channel in 1997

Channel	Total Sales	Scanner Volume	Scan % of Sales
Grocery	337	293	87%
Convenience	82	21	26%
Club	44	44	100%
Discount	120	119	99%
Drug	42	24	57%
Super center	46	40	87%
TOTAL for non-grocery	334	248	74%

Note: Dollars are in billions and valued in 1997 dollars.
Source: Information Resources, Inc.

Exhibit 7: Soft Benefits Realized to Date

Category	Savings (% of Sales)	Savings ($ Billions)	Notes
DSD & shrink control	.60%	$1.76	Estimates based on original case. Only improvements in DSD and shrink realized.
Value of U.P.C. data and data analysis	.29%	$.85	Used annual sales for IRI, A. C. Nielsen, and smaller firms as proxy for value
Efficient replenishment	2.00%	$5.86	Warehouse, transportation, and order processing costs represent 10% of sales. E&Y estimates that ER has resulted in improvements to date ranging between 15% and 35%. Using 20% as a conservative estimate, 20% * 10% = 2%
TOTAL	2.89% of sales	$8.47 billion	Original estimate was .15% of sales or $440 million

Exhibit 8: Evolution of Benefits ($ Millions)

	1973 Original Forecast	1975 Business Case	1997* Productivity Industry Size Same – 1975 Dollars	1997* Productivity Industry Size Same – 1997 Dollars	1997 Size of Grocery* Industry and Degree of Implementation
Net benefits from U.P.C.					
Hard benefits	36	120	430	1,101	8,070
Soft benefits	18	23	451	1,155	8,470
TOTAL	54	143	881	2,256	16,540
Net HARD Benefits from U.P.C.					
Hard savings	312	488	539	1,380	10,115
Hard costs	276	368	109	279	2,045
Hard benefits	36	120	430	1,101	8,070
Net SOFT benefits from U.P.C.					
Soft savings	40	45	537	1,375	10,083
Soft costs	22	23	86	220	1,613
Soft Benefits	18	22	451	1,155	8,470

*Benefits realized have been estimated by taking the same methodology used by McKinsey & Co. in 1973 and applying the methodology to the grocery industry in 1997.

CONTRIBUTORS

David K. Allison is Chairman of the Division of Information Technology and Society, National Museum of American History. His division encompasses museum collections and exhibitions in the area of computers, mathematics, printing and graphic arts, photography, electricity, modern physics and numismatics. Dr. Allison's particular specialty is history of modern digital computers.

Prior to joining the Smithsonian staff in 1987, Dr. Allison served as a historian for the Department of Energy, and historian of naval research and development for the Department of the Navy.

Dr. Allison has a Ph.D. in History of Science from Princeton University.

David Carlson joined Sagence Systems, Inc. in July 1999 as president and C.E.O.

Prior to joining Sagence, Carlson served as senior vice president and chief technology officer of Ingram Micro, Inc., the world's largest wholesale provider of technology products and services.

Carlson is the former president of Customer Focused Technology, Inc. Before holding this position, he was vice president of technology and network services for FTD Corporation. He also served as senior vice president, chief information officer for Kmart Corporation.

John T. Dunlop is Lamont University Professor Emeritus at Harvard University and editor of the Wertheim Publications in Industrial Relations. He served as Director of the Cost of Living Council (wage and price controls), 1973–1974, for President Nixon, and as Secretary of Labor in President Ford's administration, 1975–1976.

Alan L. Haberman has had long and continuing interest in the field of automatic identification, in which the U.P.C. was a pioneer and continues to play a leadership role. While President and C.E.O. of First National Stores, Inc. he served on the Ad Hoc Committee for a Uniform Grocery Product Code and chaired its Symbol Selection Committee. He has been a member of the Board of Governors of the UCC since its inception in 1974, and is now its longest sitting member. He is chairman of the Sub-committee on Automatic Identification and Data Capture Techniques (SC31) of the Joint Technical Committee 1 (JTC1) sponsored by the International Organization for Standards (ISO) and the International Electrotechnical Commission (IEC). He served as Chairman of the Board of Overseers of the MIT Auto-ID Center, pro tem through June 15, 2001. He was co-chair of the organizing committee for the "Twenty-five Years Behind Bars" symposium.

Marvin L. Mann, chairman emeritus of Lexmark International, Inc. and its parent company, Lexmark International Group, Inc., has more than thirty years of diverse executive experience including his former position as vice president of IBM. He served as chairman from Lexmark's founding in 1991 until April 29, 1999, and was chief executive officer from 1991 to 1998. Mann, who has experience in marketing, finance, product, and general management, was instrumental in the formation of Lexmark.

Mann is a member of the board of directors of Dynatech Corporation, the M. A. Hanna Company, and Imation Corporation and a member of the Fidelity Investments board of trustees. He holds a bachelor's degree in accounting and economics from Samford University in Birmingham, Alabama and a master's degree in marketing and economics from the University of Alabama.

Bob L. Martin, who joined Wal-Mart in 1984 after a fifteen-year career with Little Rock, Arkansas-based Dillard Department Stores, served as C.E.O. of the company's international division from 1993 until June of 1999.

Before joining the international division, Martin served as Wal-Mart's chief information officer and was instrumental in the development of the company's advanced information systems. He led the development and operation of Wal-Mart's advanced technological capabilities.

John E. Nelson, who joined PricewaterhouseCoopers in 1997, leads the firm's consumer and industrial products consulting practice in the Midwest region. He specializes in implementations of ERP systems for *Fortune* 500 organizations.

An experienced consultant, Nelson has experience in managing teams of software package developers, managing alliances between organizations and international business, having lived in the U.S., Canada, the U.K., and Australia.

He received a bachelor's degree in business and computer science from Western Illinois University.

Ronald L. Nicol is a senior vice president at The Boston Consulting Group's (BCG) and leader of the organization's worldwide high technology and telecommunications practice.

Nicol received a bachelor's of science degree in physics with honors from the United States Naval Academy where he was awarded the Congressional Medal of Honor Society Prize for outstanding engineering work. He received a master's degree in business administration from Duke University, where he was named Fuqua Scholar.

Lawrence C. Russell played an essential role in the development of the U.P.C. as a McKinsey & Company consultant to the Ad Hoc Committee. His extensive career also includes management consulting at The Boston Consulting Group, senior line management responsibilities with The First National Bank of Chicago, and the presidency of the Unisys Information Services Group.

Russell earned a bachelor's degree in mechanical engineering from Lehigh University, a master's degree in business administration from Western Reserve University and a J.D. from Cleveland Marshall Law School.

Ted Rybeck is the founder of Surgency, Inc. (was Benchmarking Partners), an innovator of benchmarking methodologies for demand and supply chain information systems. He currently teaches at the Massachusetts Institute of Technology where he created a course for executive and graduate students titled, "Developing the C.E.O. Team's Value Chain Network Strategy." He also writes extensively on demand and supply chain strategies.

Before founding Benchmarking Partners, Rybeck directed all research operations for Advanced Manufacturing Research (AMR). He holds a bachelor's degree in economics from Haverford College.

Craig Schnuck is chairman and C.E.O. of Schnuck Markets, Inc.

A former chairman of the board of govenors for the Uniform Code Council, Inc., Schnuck played a key role in guiding the organization toward global initiatives and the electronic business commerce of the future.

Schnuck earned a bachelor's degree in food distribution and a master's of business administration from Cornell University.

Thomas W. Wilson, Jr. headed the consumer package goods practice at McKinsey and Company from 1970 to 1990. Beginning in 1971, Tom and his team worked closely with the Ad Hoc Committee, toward the development of the U.P.C. code and symbol. He continued as a consultant to the UCC until 1989, during which time he helped focus the council on building its strengths, husbanding its resources, and developing its reputation so as to be well prepared for growth. Tom has also played a definitive role in the creation of EAN, the formation of VICS, and the expansion of the ubiquitous global role of the U.P.C. He is chairman of the executive committee of Information Resources Inc., which provides U.P.C.-based, point of sale information to the consumer package goods industry. He is also a chairman and director of Productivity Solutions Inc., builder of point of sale equipment for customer self-checkout.

Published by Harvard University Press

J. D. Houser, *What the Employer Thinks,* 1927

Wertheim Lectures on Industrial Relations, 1929

William Haber, *Industrial Relations in the Building Industry,* 1930

Johnson O'Connor, *Psychometrics,* 1934

Paul H. Norgren, *The Swedish Collective Bargaining System,* 1941

Leo C. Brown, S.J., *Union Policies in the Leather Industry,* 1947

Walter Galenson, *Labor in Norway,* 1949

Dorothea de Schweinitz, *Labor and Management in a Common Enterprise,* 1949

Ralph Altman, *Availability for Work: A Study in Unemployment Compensation,* 1950

John. T. Dunlop and Arthur D. Hill, *The Wage Adjustment Board: Wartime Stabilization in the Building and Construction Industry,* 1950

Walter Galenson, *The Danish System of Labor Relations: A Study in Industrial Peace,* 1952.

Lloyd H. Fisher, *The Harvest Labor Market in California,* 1953

Donald J. White, *The New England Fishing Industry: A Study in Price and Wage Setting,* 1954

Val R. Lorwin, *The French Labor Movement,* 1954

George B. Baldwin, *Beyond Nationalization: The Labor Problems of British Coal,* 1955

Kenneth F. Walker, *Industrial Relations in Australia,* 1956

Charles A. Myers, *Labor Problems in the Industrialization of India,* 1958

Herbert J. Spiro, *The Politics of German Codetermination,* 1958

Mark W. Leiserson, *Wages and Economic Control in Norway, 1945–1957,* 1959

J. Pen, *The Wage Rate under Collective Bargaining,* 1959

Jack Stieber, *The Steel Industry Wage Structure: A Study of the Joint Union-Management Job Evaluation Program in the Basic Steel Industry,* 1959

Theodore V. Purcell, S.J., *Blue Collar Man: Patterns of Dual Allegiance, in Industry,* 1960

Carl Erik Knoellinger, *Labor in Finland,* 1960

Sumner H. Slichter, *Potentials of the American Economy, Selected Essays,* edited by John T. Dunlop, 1961

C. L. Christenson, *Economic Redevelopment in Bituminous Coal: The Special Case of Technological Advance in the United States Coal Mines, 1930–1960,* 1962

Daniel L. Horowitz, *The Italian Labor Movement,* 1963

Adolf Sturmthal, *Workers Councils: A Study of Workplace Organization on Both Sides of the Iron Curtain,* 1964

Vernon H. Jensen, *Hiring of Dock Workers and Employment Practices in the Ports of New York, Liverpool, London, Rotterdam, and Marseilles,* 1964

John L. Blackman, Jr., *Presidential Seizure in Labor Disputes,* 1957

Mary Lee Ingbar and Lester D. Taylor, *Hospital Costs in Massachusetts: An Economic Study,* 1968

Keneth F. Walker, *Australian Industrial Relations Systems,* 1970

David Kuechle, *The Story of the Savannah: An Episode in Maritime Labor-Management Relations,* 1971

Studies in Labor-Management History

Lloyd Ulman, *The Rise of the National Trade Union: The Development and Significance of Its Structure, Governing Institutions, and Economic Policies,* second edition, 1955

Joseph P. Goldberg, *The Maritime Story: A Study in Labor-Management Relations, 1957,* 1958

Walter Galenson, *The CIO Challenge to the AFL: A History of the American Labor Movement, 1935–1941,* 1960

Morris A. Horowitz, *The New York Hotel Industry: A Labor Relations Study,* 1960

Mark Perlman, *The Machinists: A New Study in American Trade Unionism,* 1961

Fred C. Munson, *Labor Relations in the Lithographic Industry,* 1963

Garth L. Mangum, *The Operating Engineers: The Economic History of a Trade Union,* 1964

David Brody, *The Butcher Workmen: A Study of Unionization,* 1964

F. Ray Marshall, *Labor in the South,* 1967

Philip Taft, *Labor Politics American Style: The California State Federation of Labor,* 1968

Walter Galenson, *The United Brotherhood of Carpenters: The First Hundred Years,* 1983

Distributed by Harvard University Press

Martin Segal, *The Rise of the United Association: National Unionism in the Pipe Trades, 1884–1924,* 1969

Arch Fredric Blakey, *The Florida Phosphate Industry: A History of the Development and Use of a Vital Mineral,* 1973

George H. Hildebrand and Garth L. Mangum, *Capital and Labor in American Copper, 1845–1990: Linkages between Product and Labor Markets,* 1991

Clark Kerr and Paul D. Staudolar, Editors, *Labor Economics and Industrial Relations,* 1994

Stephen A. Brown, *Revolution at the Checkout Counter: The Explosion of the Bar Code,* 1997

Alan L. Haberman, General Editor, *Twenty-five Years Behind Bars,* 2001